EARTH
MAGIC

EARTH MAGIC

A Wisewoman's Guide to Herbal,
Astrological, and Other Folk Wisdom

CLAIRE NAHMAD

Destiny Books
Rochester, Vermont

Destiny Books
One Park Street
Rochester, Vermont 05767

Library of Congress Cataloging-in-Publication Data
Nahmad, Claire.
    Earth magic : a wisewoman's guide to herbal, astrological, and other folk wisdom / Claire Nahmad.
        p. cm.
    Includes index.
    ISBN 0-89281-424-1
    1. Withcraft. 2. Magic, Celtic. 3. Astrology. 4. Plants—Folklore. 5. Religious calendars—Paganism. 6. Women—Religious life. I. Title
    BF1566.N34   1993
    133.4'3—dc20   93-14132
                                            CIP

Printed and bound in the United States

10 9 8 7 6 5 4 3

Text Design by Virginia Scott

Destiny Books is a division of Inner Traditions International

Earth Magic

is dedicated to my daughter,

Rebecca Fay Nahmad,

who is the next to inherit

CONTENTS

ACKNOWLEDGMENTS

I welcome this opportunity to acknowledge my debt to Peter Lemesurier for the many insights provided by his book *Gospel of the Stars* (Compton Press 1977); to Joan Hodgson, co-editor of Stella Polaris, for the enlightenment provided by her astrological articles; to Stephen Verney for his essay on St. George in his book *Into the New Age;* and to my editor Tessa Strickland for her part in the genesis of *Earth Magic* and for her inspiration, encouragement, and enthusiasm throughout.

INTRODUCTION

There is a strange and beautiful nighttime phenomenon, only occasionally to be seen in the northern hemisphere, called the zodiacal light. In springtime, it is just a glow in the western skies after the sun has set and gone. In the autumn, it can be seen in the east before sunrise, like a radiant mist with a pearly luster set at its heart. But in the tropics its conical shape expands into a ring of light like a crown, some parts of it as brilliant as the stars. For those who believe that life has meaning and that no phenomenon is senseless or random, this haunting light may seem to be a celebration of the zodiac itself, its stars and planets, the sun and moon that majestically tread its course, and the unending and unfathomable significance it has for our beloved earth, the exquisite center-jewel of the universe as we experience it.

Earth Magic is written from this perspective. My material is drawn from the ancient wisewoman's tradition, a tradition that reaches back many centuries to a time when the influence of the stars and planets on all animate and inanimate things of the earth was acknowledged and accepted, and when practitioners of healing and herbalism, whose vision was holistic, took these influences into account and were expert in their understanding of them. Despite the ascendancy of an over-rational emphasis on medicine and science, despite the persecution of women during the witch hunts of sixteenth-century Europe, despite the poor regard in which astrology is now held, this lore has been passed down in the oral tradition of womenfolk for generation after generation.

Much of it has been relayed faithfully from century to century by simple country people, as well as being recorded in detail by great men of science such as Copernicus, Galileo, and St. Thomas Aquinas. Both sources contribute to our western mystery tradition.

This verbal lore of the wisewoman teaches us how to love and revere the earth, how to respond to her magic and return in some measure the blessing and healing that we receive from her. It is a tradition that acknowledges sexual equality, values the significance of the inner life, and respects the liberty of the individual. At its heart is a mystical vision of the universe in which the earth is seen as spirit and her brothers and sisters in the solar system as the physical counterparts of great spiritual beings. Our evolution as human beings is believed to affect the evolution of the earth spirit, which, in turn, affects the evolution of even mightier beings; the same principle assures us that the animal and plant kingdoms need our assistance in advancing their own evolution, and even that we are connected through this integrated chain to the mineral kingdom in which the herbs and trees and grasses have their roots. Many will instinctively feel the truth of this, having loved the scents of the wholesome brown soil and felt the life and mystery, even the beating heart, in stones and rocks and precious jewels.

The moon is the first astrological planet, and her deep significance and influence on our lives is revealed symbolically through the myth of Endymion, the shepherd who is humanity, with whom the moon fell in love as he lay asleep on the hillside. She set out to enchant him so that his awareness of her would unite their souls during the day as well as at night.

The moon's tides evoke a daily and monthly cycle of growth in the nature kingdom and in the movement of the animals. Dogs are associated with the moon, and her radiant fullness evokes howling and other forms of moon-worship among them.

Not only the moon but all of the planets and their conjunctions affect life on earth. All the light coming from deep space is electromagnetic, and the universe can be understood as being an electromagnetic network, governed by the constant fusing of the god (electro) and goddess (magnetic) principles. This includes our own magnetosphere, the field of energy that surrounds the earth. The scientists of today confirm what the wisewoman's tradition has known intuitively for centuries: that the macrocosmic atom that is our earth is reflected microcosmically in all her life; every cell of every manifest body is also surrounded by a similar energy field. In the same way, every cell in every organism has, and gives, access to the influences or information contained in the electromagnetic spacefield. Accordingly, each planetary radiation sparks off impulses that reverberate within the biocell and initiate a pattern of predetermined development.

When the planets pass through the solar electromagnetic field, the radiation of their own energies combines with that of the sun to create electromagnetic waves. These, when in adverse aspect to one another and to the earth, are the cause of intense radioactive disturbance. The planetary stresses, positive and negative, are therefore recorded on earth; yet, as human beings, we are all invested with the divine power to rise above the negative pull that binds us to the earthly planes and to harmonize the incoming planetary influences within the magical crucible of our own being.

There are two zodiacs (an Arabic word meaning "circle of animals"). The first is an imaginary division of space into a ring or crown of twelve equal arcs that mark out the ecliptic, the apparent path of the sun as, seen from "below" on earth, it appears to move around our planet. The second consists of twelve constellations. The correspondence between the two is one of creative or inspired imagination as well as precise measurement. The sun is an important influence in any astrological chart, but its power is subtly matched by the moon. Each month, she moves from sign to sign through each of the twelve constellations, completing her journey through all twelve signs in approximately twenty-nine days and spending about two and a half days in each. Her position in the universe, in relation to the signs of earth, water, fire and air, influences life on earth with a mysterious and delicate touch.

Beyond our solar system particular stars relate to certain types of persons, beasts, plants, and stones, so that "star-families" appear on Earth, dying away as the star declines so that new stars may give subtle birth. Knowledge of the inspiration coming from the stars helps us to revere them, not as austere and distant objects but as beings with whom we can make warm and human soul-contact.

Through the wisewoman's tradition, we can appreciate the ever-changing influence of the stars on our lives and on all the plants and creatures with whom we are privileged to share our world. We may learn from the women of old the mystery in the folkname of a flower; the strange and lovely myths associated with trees; the fabulous tales told of totem beasts, which are symbols of our inner selves; the magical attributes of birds; the phantoms of the old gods seen in clouds and weather phenomena; the spirits perceived in wells and running water, in fairy hills and halls. Our heritage is rich indeed, and the treasury of spells, charms, tales, beliefs, herbal lore, and underworld wisdom spun through the years and handed down from age to age enshrines and shelters the golden and silver threads of pattern and meaning that enrich all of our lives.

The "wisewoman" of the text is not me, but I was fortunate to inherit, as a child, the traditional wisdom of the craft from my maternal grandmother. The wisewoman's voice may be regarded as the voice of an ancient wisdom whose wellsprings are fed by Britain's druidic past. While they boast no high esoteric knowledge (although such knowledge was surely an attainment of ancient cultures), the wisewoman's teachings are permeated with a gentle vision that may help us to realize once again that the earth is indeed magical.

NOTE
ON THE TEXT

The meditations and invocations on the angels of the spheres and the planets, as given, are by no means meant rigidly to dictate concepts of the form and manifestation of angels—which would be a fool's endeavor—but are intended only as guidelines, a starting point for inspiration and meditation personal to you; the "spirits" of the planets are more correctly their "souls" or, rather, the sum total of those qualities that the ancient astrologers associated with them; the angels behind or above the planets are mighty beings concerned with the whole spectrum of life rather than the attainment and growth of the individual. This does not mean, however, that it is not right to seek to draw near to the angels, for they will bless us and teach us if we ask in the right way. To absorb the qualities generated by the planets it is useful to concentrate on them and call them by name, but it is always wise to ask the blessing of the planetary angel, too.

While the use of charms, herbal medicine, and communion with the angels in the event of illness is recommended, it is also most important that you should consult your doctor, so that he or she can advise you on your condition and monitor it. To ensure your recognition of the star groups (some of which intermingle), it is advisable to obtain star maps (often available at a bookstore or stationary store). It is worth the trouble of procuring these, because familiarity with the stars begins to open the door upon a very beautiful awareness of our earth as a member of the holistic universe. It does not lead to a feeling of individual insignificance and loneliness but to a consciousness that banishes feelings of isolation.

When emerging from meditation, it is highly recommended for your own safety and comfort that you "seal the chakras." These seven inner gateways are situated in our corporeal body at the crown, the brow, the throat, the heart, the spleen, the solar plexus, and the base of the spine. Just think of a silver cross encircled with light and seal each center with this symbol as soon as you are ready to come out of meditation. Now draw a spiral of light around your body from your toes to the top of your head, using your creative imagination. Let it enfold you seven times, and then "earth" yourself by mentally summoning the light right down through the center of the spiral to your feet.

If for some reason you happen at any time to be unable to go through the entire sealing process, at least direct the silver cross in its circle of light to blaze out upon your brow, throat and solar plexus centers before resuming daily life. When sitting in meditation, you will find it helpful if you place your right ankle across your left and cup your left hand in your right (esoteric lore tells us we receive with the left hand and give with the right).

The frequent references to "Christ" in the text are not meant to exclude any religion or those who have none. It simply means "the true light" and every soul who loves Mother Earth will know well what that means.

Chapter One

MARCH

The Reawakening

Spring Paean

Give praise to the Dagda, Father of all, Lord of Boundless Knowledge, giver of life and of death; in the depths of his sacred halls he makes music on his magic harp, strange and lovely as the voices of faery birds, which flies to the heart of the deep-breasted earth, there to call forth into being the round of the seasons; so that forever do they dance back and forth from the stars.

Celtic fable

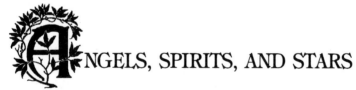

NGELS, SPIRITS, AND STARS

Across the heavens stretches the Grand Man of the Stars, walking the celestial spheres with his great legs astride and his giant's arms extended above his head so that he forms a diagonal cross. He is circumscribed by the turning wheel of the skies, and bears upon his body the inscriptions of the planets and the symbols of the zodiac. The central point of the cross he makes forms his solar plexus, where the heavenly spiritual influences unite with the earthly energies emanating from below.

The planet Mars is one of the rulers of the three earthly centers on the great map of consciousness that is the zodiac. He is the ruler of Aries, the first sign of the zodiac and the exaltation of the sun.

The Grand Man of the Stars has been associated from ancient times with the Dagda, the great Celtic God of All who brought into being the four seasons as he played his magical harp. Indeed, poetry and science merge as we consider that it is not unlikely that the stars (together with the power of our sun) do bring the seasons, the magnitude of their power like the tides of the sea pounding with life upon the shores of earth and then receding, withdrawing, true to the cycle of the cosmic breath.*

The fiery energy of the planet Mars ushers in those beating cosmic tides, stirring after the winter solstice, breaking free in February, and finally harmonizing in March, to which Mars lends his name as he triumphantly heralds the spring. The Mars energy is in all nature as it begins to bud and burst forth; Arian people generally feel this burning drive throughout their lives, inspiring them always to active achievement and upward striving. The little chick valiantly battling its way out of the egg is enthused with the spirit of Mars. There is a deeper lesson here, too, because although Mars stampedes throughout our earthly nature in all his glory, his final mission is to release us from the shell of fierce emotionalism, of earthly desires and their limitations—the battleground of our struggle with this warrior—and to help to lift us into enlightenment.

Mars is the god of war, the spirit of conquest, one of the twelve major Olympian deities. Son of Zeus and Hera and lover of Venus, Mars is associated with dryness, fire, great heat, and masculine energy. The planet itself can be seen at night as a "star" of a brilliant reddish hue, in keeping with its symbolism. Interestingly enough, Mars is actually this color because it is rusty! This points to Mars's association with the watery Scorpio, which speaks of renunciation and sacrifice; so is Mars's aridity tempered by the mercy of rain and moisture. Considering this it is not so surprising to learn that Bride, or Bridget, goddess of

----

* Science explains the round of the seasons by the fact that the earth's polar axis is at right angles to the plane of its orbit around the sun at equinox positions and is tilted at the greatest angle at the time of the solstices.

the new moon and spirit of fire and poetry, is the balancing feminine principle, the woman aspect, of Mars in Celtic tradition. It may be that Mars, as the lover of Venus, has a deeper, more spiritual nature in Bride and sounds an inherent promise that his fiery and independent path must culminate in balance, beauty, and ultimate truth.

Without the vigor and pace of Mars, without his heated desire to succeed, we would find ourselves incapable of garnering the gifts of the gods. We can draw consciously on Martian energy, calling upon his soldiering spirit for inspiration and absorbing his power whenever the need arises; yet it is wise to seek always to balance this leaping power with wisdom and gentleness and essential humanity, because raw Martian exuberance can work against these qualities.

As an initiator of the seasons, and as representative of an aspect of the Dagda influence, it is interesting that Mars, the planet, has a rotation of four seasons, its own hemispheres alternating between summer and winter in the same way those of our earth do. The Dagda harp might even be thought of as the Lyre, that beautiful star cluster visible on clear spring nights just after midnight on the eastern horizon in the month of March. A harp or lyre appearing in the skies at midnight (the hour of profound secrets and magic), a symbol of the recurring cycle of days, seasons, and years, is too potent a coincidence to ignore, especially when it is observed that this appearance of the Lyre constellation in the eastern skies (a sacred position for stars), and at midnight, occurs only in March.

The planetary archangel ruling Mars is the Archangel Samael, who has his or her correspondence in gods and myths and celestial winged beings of many cultures. This planetary angel balances and harmonizes the raw force of Mars and his animating spirit. Samael may be called upon to bless any endeavors involving the use of machinery. He/she grants courage, endurance, fortitude and will give protection and guidance in respect of fires and situations that threaten sudden violence, either from the natural world or from human encounters.*

*Angels represent the balance of both sexes; they may be both male and female or one or the other, according to the need of the percipient.

Zodiac

ARIES—RAM
MARCH 21–APRIL 19

ANGEL: Archangel Samael

RULING PLANET: Mars

KEYWORD: Appearance—that which is imminent, immanent, originating, the creativity of strength

AGE: Womanhood (28–35 years)
Manhood (28–35 years)

METAL: Iron

CROSS: Cardinal (the Mother)

ELEMENT: Fire

QUALITIES: Forceful, self-willed, enthusiastic, exaggerative, passionate, extrovert, pioneer, courageous, self-sufficient, idealistic

ILLNESSES TO GUARD AGAINST: Fevers, inflammatory complaints, wounds, accidents

BODY AREAS: Head, brain, face

STONES: Ruby, bloodstone, diamond, garnet

NUMBERS: 7 and 9

DAY: Tuesday

FLOWERS AND HERBS: Thistle, wild rose, gorse, nasturtium, woodbine, wake-robin

TREES: Holly, thorn, chestnut

ANIMALS: Ram, tiger, leopard, stallion, vulture

BIRDS: Magpie, robin

COLOR: Red—all bright colors are harmonious for the Aries person, especially green, pink, white, and yellow

Aries is named after the ram bearing the Golden Fleece sought by Jason and the Argonauts.

Meditation on Mars

We may imagine Mars as the great forger, his the workshop of life, the smithy. An aspect of Mars is the northern deity, the mighty thunder-god, Thor.

The alchemists ruled that alchemical works should be initiated when the sun was in Aries, Taurus, or Gemini—in other words, at some point during the spring. Our own "alchemical works," mundane or artistic, simple or stupendous, need springtime energies at their inauguration. At the start of any new project or enterprise, or when energies are running low and we feel the need to call on qualities of bravery, determination, and stamina, this invocation to Mars may be worked; in conjunction, it is wise to call on angelic assistance, a communion of a deeper, more personal and spiritual nature, to be guided by individual intuition.

Light a red candle at one of the hours of Samael—between six and seven in the morning, two and three in the afternoon, and ten and eleven o'clock at night. These three hours are sacred to the planetary angel of Mars, and it is as well to use them, although a supplication to the Mars being or spirit can be used at any time when the need for his influences and energy arises.

You may like to dress the candle by rubbing into the wax a rose oil to balance the Mars power with his feminine aspect, secreted at his heart. Intone the following words, speaking from the seat of your deeper consciousness (not the frontal mind of the intellect), the mind in the heart, which is activated by means of the spirit working through the higher or creative imagination.

> Mars, warrior of the heart, spirit of dynamism, courage, and vitality, protector and energizer of the weak and the fearful, I conjure your robust presence before me. I see you now as a glorious being enrobed in bright red, the color of passionate blood racing with all the joy and zest of vernal energy, casting out fear and charging all depletion with new life; and the color also of the red rose, signifying the magical presence of the heart of Venus, giving forth love and sweetness and poising your martial strength in the radiance of

harmony. I see your plumed helmet, your red hair and beard flowing underneath it; I see your eyes like undying embers glowing with the fire of the stars, flashing with the impulses of regeneration, the thrust of the will of new life. I see your Chief's Wand, denoting the power to triumph; your sword at your belt, ever ready to protect and drive back the foe; your shield, glittering and valiant, which has the power to resist all malignant and invading forces.

I ask you to enthuse me with your knowledge, your powers, your fearlessness and enterprise and all the soul-qualities I have named and depicted; so that I go from this place armored and brilliant and infused with your inspiration, guided always by the light of my own spirit, which is a particle of the heart of the Great Spirit of All whose Love, Wisdom, and Power illumines my path.

Stars of Spring

Look for Leo in the night skies of springtime. It is a striking group of stars, east, west, or on the meridian itself, according to the earliness or lateness of the hour and the season. The constellation has two parts: on the right-hand side a curve of stars called the Sickle because of the likeness it bears to the old-fashioned farming tool, and on the left-hand side a group of stars in the form of a triangle. In between there is a gap in which faint stars shine. The Sickle consists of six stars, the lowest of which is Regulus ("little king") or Alpha Leonis, also called Rex, Basilikus, Malikiyy ("the kingly") by Copernicus, Ptolemy, and the Arabs, respectively. Inscriptions in the Euphrates valley call it the "star of the king," and the ancient Persians recognized it as the chief of the four royal stars.

If you observe with patience, you will begin to discern the different hues of the stars without the aid of binoculars or a telescope. These delicate star colors are one of the delights of star gazing.

The wisewoman says of the stars:

> Find time to go out in the dark of the night and watch the stars. They will become familiar to you, even as friends and comforters. You will feel you are known to them, that they greet you with a tender effusion of love and brotherliness. They cannot but gladden your heart if you will seek to gaze upon them nightly and establish this as a ritual. You will learn much, much of what is so secret it cannot be spoken, much that is the voice of the secrets in your own heart, that nothing else can reveal to you in this world except the stars.
>
> Do not think you can know the meaning of the stars, or learn their wisdom, by giving ear to men of science. If what you learn by study and scholarship causes your wonder and love of the stars and your reverence for their marvels and beauty to grow, then such scholarship is well for you. But should that recognition of their magic be diminished, should you once begin to think that you can hold the firmament in your own little head, which is like a planet's egg, lowly and unhatched, then beware; their secrets, their wisdom, their songs will be lost to you, and you will begin to turn into a creature of clay.
>
> There are songs of the stars and dances of the stars, and these you must learn. The stars will teach you. The time will come when you are not able to resist the dance of the stars. When you dance the dance of the stars, you begin to learn that each and every star sounds its note in the great symphony of nature here below on our good earth.

Lady Day

Lady Day, March 25, marks the festival of the Annunciation, the announcement of the Incarnation made by the angel Gabriel to the Virgin Mary.

Esoteric Christianity suggests that the life of Christ was a great cosmic drama enacted on earth in human terms; from this viewpoint it is interesting to note that Gabriel is the angel of the moon, so intimately associated with the mother goddess; the Virgin Mary represents virgin matter, a sacred receptacle for the nurturing of the spirit (the Christ child).

Tibetan Buddhism claims that our world is a goddess world (the world of Shakti) and that the mother aspect of the godhead is reflected through the principles of matter and form. It is her "project," so to speak. This seems to elucidate the belief that humanity descended into matter from the highest realms of divine spirit, in order that matter might be gathered into the light of that spirit (a term for matter was *dark Egypt*, meaning bodies that gave forth no light).

It might be helpful as a meditation for Lady Day to imagine the Great Goddess enrobed in madonna blue, the eternal waters of the causal ocean of life swirling around her feet and the moon as her diadem. Her hands gently cradle the light cascading from the shining star that is her heart as she contemplates the divine radiance of spirit.

Feel the caring, nurturing, gentle qualities of the Great Goddess, the sweetness and the mystery that she emanates . . . . and particularly feel her *power,* the goddess power behind all manifest life.

 ISEWOMAN'S JOURNAL

Now here is a method to soothe you into sleep. In your mind's eye, count the playful lambs as they make sport in the springtime fields; and count them the way the shepherd does it:

> Yan, tan, tethera, pethera, pimp, sethera, lethera, hovera, covera, dik, yan-a-dik, tan-a-dik, tethera-dik, pethera-dik, bumfit, yan-a-bumfit, tan-a-bumfit, tethera-bumfit, pethera-bumfit, figgit.

Spring Amulet

If, in the months of spring, you can find a place where oak, ash, and thorn grow close together, that is especially lucky, and the place is blessed. Ask leave of each of the trees and break off from old man oak, old woman thorn, and the "ever-young and immortal ash who bears the weight of the world" one twig each, with the buds just swelling and showing green. Bind them with red thread so that the thorn and the ash are crossed and the oak is upright behind them. Say this as you work:

> Ash wand of immortality
> Oak staff strong and holy
> Blossoming bough that bears the may
> Three together I bind this day
> To make sign of Blessed Trinity.
> Oak the father, hawthorn mother,
> Ash the child of ancient spring
> From harms of earth and sky and sea and fire
> May your magic wood protection bring.

Then you will have all year round a powerful amulet against every trouble and sorrow the world can bring; and even should they enter your house, you will be strengthened in courage and fortitude, so that they retreat again over your threshold.

Author's Note

It is noteworthy that the oak is sacred to the Druids, the ancient priesthood of the British Isles and beyond, and that their goddess of the may was the earth-mother goddess who was also queen of heaven. In this context, the "child of ancient spring" who "bears the weight of the world" is revealed as the eternal source of renewal, or the archetypal Christ figure in nature. Yggdrasil, the world-tree (of Norse mythology), the magical nature. Yggdrasil, the world-tree (of Norse mythology), the magical inner structure of the planet and the mystical nature of humanity, always green and in its springtime flourish of growth is represented as the ash. The cosmology of the Druids was also conceived as a divine and immortal tree, the oak being its sign and symbol.

Mother Henbane's Fragrant Charm Bag for Friendship and Happiness

Gather these herbs at the first light of dawn on a fine spring morning; choose a time when the moon is between new and its first week of waxing; if you can, do the working on a Friday, which is the day of Venus, and wear around your waist a green girdle, even if this be hid under your clothes:

Sweet violets	Lavender leaves	Leaves and flowers
Comfrey	Green moss	of Rosemary
Dandelion heads	Daisies	Elderflowers or leaves
Primrose	Thyme	Sage
Ivy leaves	Groundsel	Horse-chestnut

Dry all these, taking care to be thorough. Then pound them well in your mortar and pestle, chanting this rune the while:

Venus flowers, flowers of the Sun
Herbs of Jupiter and old Saturn
I pound and grind to make as one.

Angels of the stars, Angels of the Hours,
With my heart I pray you, bless these flowers;
Harmony, friendship, delight, and joy
Seal herein by magic's employ.

Round and round you must go with this spell, so that the herbs be deeply charmed. Wash and dry a white cotton handkerchief as a holy ritual. Make up in the same way a little bag of the white cotton, dividing the material into four parts, one bag for each square. Your own sewing and embroidery is good, but it must be done in pure white silken thread, or one that is dyed in rose-pink.

Put the ground herbs and flowers into the bags and place in each a tiny white pebble no bigger than a pearl, which you will discover by digging into the earth; a brand new farthing; and a little powdered orris root. Tie the neck of each bag sharp and tight with rose-pink cord or ribbon. Do this at Auriel's evening hour, which is between eight and nine of the clock.

On the next Thursday of the waxing moon, take a blue candle, light it again at Auriel's evening hour, having anointed it with rose oil, and chant this spell:

> Friendship, gladness, heart's delight
> Are my three prayers which take their flight
> On wings of incense into Sachiel's night.
>
> Auriel and Sachiel
> Angels two that hear my spell
> Friendship, gladness, heart's delight
> These treasures bring from Paradise;
> Secrete them in my deepest soul
> May my spirit keep them whole.

Finish the ceremony by thanking the angels first; then take each of the four bags, open them at the neck and stir into their magical essences one or two drops of rose oil. Pass the open bags through the smoke of the candle, or yet just above the candle flame, thanking the angels once again for their beneficence. Then tie up the bags. Leave the candle in a safe place to burn down.

The following day, Friday, take a green candle, light it once more at Auriel's hour after you have dressed it well in rose-oil, and chant again:

> Friendship, gladness, heart's delight
> Are my three prayers which take their flight
> On wings of incense into Anael's night.
>
> Auriel and Anael
> Angels two that hear my spell
> Friendship, gladness, heart's delight
> These treasures bring from Paradise;
> Secrete them in my deepest soul
> May my spirit keep them whole.

And do all again as I have told you.

The next day, Saturn's day, take an orange-brown candle, light it at Auriel's evening hour, having taken care to anoint it with the oil, and chant the spell for the last time:

> Friendship, gladness, heart's delight
> Are my three prayers which take their flight
> On wings of incense into Cassiel's night.
>
> Auriel and Cassiel
> Angels two that hear my spell
> Friendship, gladness, heart's delight
> These treasures bring from Paradise;
> Secrete them in my deepest soul
> May my spirit keep them whole.

Do all again as before; only this time you must make the magical sign ≈, which is the sign of good fellowship, in the soft wax of the candle, and you must drop a tiny droplet of it into each bag; and when you have done all with them that you should to work the spell, bind them once more for the last time, and seal them by making a cross of the wax upon the knot of the ribbon.

Now, one of these bags is for the fairies, for you need their good will; so take it to a wood or a wild place, find the hollow of a tree, and place it therein.

The second bag you must offer to the angels and the great spirit of all; and you may best accomplish this by making a gift of it to one who needs and wants the charm. The third bag is your surety against loss; place this in a secret nook in your bedchamber together with the Joker card from a Tarot pack or regular playing cards. Bind them together with another length of the ribbon you used to bind the bag, and let them lie in darkness. The fourth bag is your own fragrant charm bag for friendship and happiness, which you must wear about your person whenever you can, especially when you sleep, and when you go about your daily business.

Author's Note

A new penny will work as well as a farthing to make up the contents of your fragrant charm bag. "Holy ritual" means keeping your magical intention in mind as you work and bringing to the mundane task a sense of "mystery and sanctity as though you worked with angels," To "go round and round ... with this spell" means to continue repeating it until the task in hand is done.

Honeybee Wine for St. Patrick's Day

This wine is best made during the summer months and left to mature for drinking the following spring.

> One quart (1.14 liters) of white clover heads
> Three quarts of red clover heads
> One pound of clover honey
> One ounce of yeast
> Three tablespoons of cider vinegar
> One gallon of pure well water

Shred the petals from the flowerheads and place the petals alone in a vessel. Cover them with two quarts of water on the boil. Put a cloth well over the vessel and leave it alone for twelve hours or more.

Stir half the honey into a quart of boiling water, thinking happy and wholesome thoughts as you do it. Leave to cool and add the mixture to the flower petals. Then stir in the yeast and the cider vinegar. Put your vessel in a warm place and let it ferment for seven days, asking the angels of the week, which are Michael, Gabriel, Samael, Raphael, Sachiel, Anael, and Cassiel, to bless it in turn, working from Sunday to Saturday.

Now make a syrup with the rest of the honey as you did before, using a quart of boiling water. Let it cool and add it to the wine in the vessel. Leave all alone again for a day, then strain the wine and leave it in peace until it ferments no more. When foam rises to the top, take it off. You have brewed your Honeybee Wine, and a fine remedy you will find it for all afflictions of the lungs. It promotes bodily purity and will refresh you throughout the lovely summer days, bringing their fragrant memories back to you in the dark depths of the drear winter.

It will help you to sleep and give you dreams as magnanimous as the happy honeybee and as mellifluent as the nectar it gathers.

Author's Note

St. Patrick, to whom the wine is dedicated, is celebrated on March 17. This grand old saint would no doubt have approved of the wine, as it has the virtue of purification. An instance of St. Patrick's zeal for purification is his utterance of a prayer to banish all reptiles and amphibians from Ireland. To this day such creatures are not to be found there. St. Patrick was the son of a Christian Roman named Calpurnius and was born in Glamorgan about A.D. 387. Irish raiders transported him to Antrim when he was sixteen. He escaped and became a monk, was ordained a priest, and was entrusted by Pope Celestine I with the conversion of Ireland. He met Laoghaire, king of Ireland, who uneasily allowed him to continue with his mission. At first he struggled with the Druids, but these wise priests came to realize that the new dispensation he offered (concerning the doctrines of the Christ) was the natural progression of their own.

St. Patrick founded many religious houses, churches, and bishoprics. His extant works ("Confession" and "Letter to Coroticus") suggest an expansive and pioneering spirit. His teaching methods were simple and direct, as in the famous incident in which it is recorded that he plucked the shamrock to depict the doctrine of the Holy Trinity (clover is of the same family as the shamrock in botanical terms).

WISEWOMAN'S WEATHERBOOK

If in the evening the southern sky is rosy with red and flush-tinted clouds sailing in from the western sunset, there will be for a few days rain and sunshine and sunshine and rain, first one and then the other like the history of a little tot's day from its rising and its going to bed.

If in the evening the roses of the western sky should ride over to the east, that foretells a change of weather, and a dithering of the weather spirits for a day or two.

When the moon wears a wedding veil with a star caught in it, rain will come to bless the earth.

Cows are prophets of the summer storms. When they gather together in close little companies of three or four all across the meadow and will not graze unless they're nuzzling their neighbors, a fine thunderstorm is approaching.

Chapter Two

APRIL

The Month of the Cuckoo

Cuckoo Song

Summer is y-comen in,
Loudè sing, cuckoo!
Groweth seed and bloweth meed
And spring'th the woodè now—
Sing cuckoo!

Ewè bleateth after lamb,
Low'th after calfè cow;
Bullock starteth, buckè farteth.
Merry sing, cuckoo!

Early English

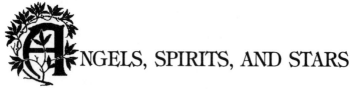

NGELS, SPIRITS, AND STARS

The constellation of Taurus, stretching across the vernal equinox and held in awe and reverence by the priests and seers of old, must have impressed their minds with its mysteries as well as its bedazzling resplendence of stars; for, at a first glance, the cosmic Bull and the

22

shining goddess of love, Venus, seem to be symbolically irreconcilable.

Taurus, the star bull, muscular, vigorous, powerful, blessed with the virtue of endurance, must lose his wings and fall to earth (the winged bull is a feature of ancient mythology); here a correspondence begins to suggest itself. For, if the starry one must fall (and we may think of Lucifer, the Bright One, and his banishment into matter), Venus as the morning star might be his appropriate symbol,* and as sign and symbol of humanity and its descent into matter, the task of the bull is clear. He has been required to renounce his pasturing in the heavenly star-meadows, and must now begin a mission of blood, sweat, and tears—he must toil and labor and, by his prodigious efforts in matter, plough the deep, narrow, perfect furrow in which to sow the treasure of the spiritual seed with all its dynamic promise of a golden harvest.

Here the symbols begin to merge. In the Far East, female genitalia have been referred to as "the furrow" and Venus is, of course, the goddess of sexual love. The symbolism fathoms depths more profound, however, than the mere representation of human mating; the old knowledge does not screech to a halt, Freudian-like, at the boundaries of sex; rather, the sexual mystery forms the frontier to boundless worlds of discovery.

For the great task of Taurus is not the simple instruction to "go forth and multiply" but the far deeper one of ushering in the physical manifestation of the exquisite harmony of the spheres. Into the heart of life on earth, into daily toil, into family life, into spheres practical, mental, emotional, and artistic, Taurus must bring down what his spirit learned when he pastured in the fiery stars. And Venus, goddess also of artistic inspiration and lover of Mars, shares an affinity with the Celtic Bride or Bridget, goddess of the new moon, of fire and poetry, and so with the starry bull. In this aspect, it would seem congruent to think of her as the Mystical Virgin, wielding spiritual power, who rides the back of a horned beast (in Celtic terms he was a unicorn, but the Taurean horns, symbol of the new moon, make the bull an equally

---

* At different times of the year, Venus is visible as the morning or the evening star; she has a host of angels of heavenly love and forgiveness, for these angels court the "star" so near to the sun. The angels of Venus surround us to help us build atoms of light in our heavy bodies of earth ("dark Egypt").

viable emblem, as is expressed in other cultures).* Taurus, signifying the physicality of humankind, must bow before the Virgin and become her vehicle, her servant and steed; and so Taurus and Venus (or the body and the spirit) are reconciled. The Beast now enjoys the love and blessing of Beauty, as the Maiden tames the Unicorn by coaxing its head into her lap. The unicorn is a symbol of purity, holistic and magical; for now Beauty and the Beast are one, which is their final destiny. The sublime soul of mankind subsumes its own lower nature.

In legend, Venus conceives a great love for the mortal Adonis, which again points to the earthly nature being visited by its higher soul. Venus was married to the ugly and morose god Vulcan. Curiously, Vulcan bears an earlier association with Volcanus, god of the thunder-bolt and of fire, and may have been in his later Vulcan personality a cruder and unbalanced version of the Martian spirit. In this context, Venus was not so much unfaithful to Vulcan because of her love for Adonis, as transformative of her husband (always depicted in ancient Roman art with a facial deformity) into the more evolved, pure and beautiful Martian being.

From such a viewpoint, the Venus/Taurus myth is lifted into a new dimension, as we reflect that not only must our human lower nature be permeated with the blessings and inspiration of the exalted soul in order that humanity as a whole may realize its full potential, but also a way may be found to achieve this by establishing a perfect equality and acceptance between the sexes—a true marriage. When Venus and Vulcan stand side by side, their balanced and harmonious union can heal the deformity in Vulcan's face (his outlook?). Myths move in dream sequences and inspired visions; the keys of individual intuition and interpretation can unlock their secrets and their wisdom and speak different truths to all who seek their teaching.

Of course, the Venus power can also be unbalanced, and when this happens, she confers unfortunate tendencies toward laziness, languid luxuriousness, and the hardhearted and selfish pursuit of self-gratifica-tion, both material and sexual; but when her influences are received

* The Greek legend of Europa and the Bull is an example, and significant in that the goddess Europa bestowed her name on Europe; "the lady and the unicorn" has been a potent mythic symbol in the West.

harmoniously, Venus bestows everything that is beautiful and gracious, fruitful and feminine, intuitive and inspirational. She gives pleasure and ease in living and creates the luster of romance. Ancient lore associates Venus with the spring. In Botticelli's, *The Birth of Venus,* she rises naked from the sea and expresses the power and magnetism inherent in woman's body, that power that the negative psychic force behind pornography seeks to corrode and corrupt. She is the keeper of a mystic girdle that has the magic to transfer her sweetness, beauty, and power to its wearer. Doves and sparrows are sacred to her, as is the soft glow of candlelight. Perfumes, too, are sacred to Venus.

Considering the Taurean association with the earth, and that of Venus with spring, it is not surprising that Taurean people should share a special relationship with the soil and all things growing in it. Gardening or walking in the country will quickly replenish them, as they are easily able to absorb life force from the earth. Martian vigor is here again associated with Venus, and it is interesting to remember that the military salute, so reminiscent nowadays of the Martian spirit, owes its origin to an ancient token of respect for the goddess. In the Dark Ages (and earlier) knights contesting in tournaments would approach the celebrated lady who had been chosen to represent the goddess, in order to receive a token whenever they were triumphant. As they accepted it, they would raise their hand as if to shield their eyes; this gesture silently communicated, "Your power and beauty dazzle me." So the salute was born.

Just as the planet Mars, rusty with the moisture of Bride, the feminine principle, reflects Venus the spirit in its physical makeup, so the planet Venus gives intimations of the Martian spirit in that its atmosphere is a living hell, smoldering with eternal fires and hostile volcanic eruptions that create a passionate physical environment of brooding red heat. Venus's beautiful and mysterious veil of pure white clouds could be seen to point to her association with the bridal veil of the goddess Bridget, or Bride; this veil also suggests the "Venetian veil," a strange phenomenon that, on rare occasions, covers newborn babies with a thin film of white skin, like a membrane, which has to be removed at birth. Such children are said to possess (and often go on to substantiate the claim) strong psychic and intuitive powers, and again this links Venus with the moon and the intuition of the psyche or the soul.

Venus's link with the moon and her conjoinment with Taurus give Taurean people the urge to build, to embody. They love to build a home, a garden, a family, a business, a group functioning within an organized framework. And so Taurus is the sign of possessions, or our human relationship to that which we create and build. Sometimes Taureans can suffer from exaggerated materialism; this arises from their unbalanced endeavors to fulfill their spiritual destiny and not because the earthy sign of Taurus is somehow more mundane and spiritually inferior to other star signs, as has been suggested.

To bring harmony and the unifying principle into matter and its structures is the destiny of the children of the starry bull. As their function is, literally, to earth the electrical current of higher inspiration from the spirit, Taureans find it difficult to let go, and so their soul and home environment can sometimes become cluttered. Strongly protective, they can react with deep consternation when the established order of life is threatened from outside. They feel a mother's bond with the edifices, mental, emotional, and physical, that they have created; likewise, they feel all the instinctive distress of a mother at the thought of having to abandon those structures to the severity of forces for change.

The moon is exalted in Taurus, and the strong association with the earth and with form expressed in matter endows Taureans with a special sensitivity toward the etheric kingdoms, the domain of the fairies. Attuned to the life force in nature, they can easily cultivate an awareness in themselves of the etheric fairy life and the work of the healing angels as they manifest their influence in the nature kingdom.

For those who feel that there is an over-strident masculinity in the gender of the star-animals, it is refreshing to consider that, in Celtic legend, the Taurean bull is often transformed into the Dun cow (*dun* means "court" in the language of the ancient Celts, suggesting that the Dun cow was considered a royal beast). Many old tales tell of this wondrous animal, a giant cow who roamed the land as guardian of it and its people, allowing herself to be milked freely. Her milk was sweet and rich and had healing properties as though it came from Paradise. This legend is part of the folklore of Ireland, England, and Wales. In each story, the heavenly cow who provides milk for the poor, especially in times of famine, is made to vanish forever by the greed and self-seeking habits of humanity. In Ireland she was abused by a woman who, wishing to take more than her fair share, milked her into a sieve. A witch did the same in the English version, taking so much milk from the poor animal that she died of exhaustion at the end of the day. A Welsh family wished to kill and eat her, so causing her magically to disappear when she heard news of it.

The Dun cow is surely a symbol for the spirit of the earth, its crops and its animals. She is simultaneously Mother Earth and the largesse that Mother Earth scatters with such a free hand and heart. In these times of factory-farmed animals and exhausted and depleted soil, it seems apposite to remember the Dun cow and the lesson offered by her legend. "The Book of the Dun Cow" (an ancient Celtic manuscript) establishes her as a guardian spirit and a sacred animal, identifying her with the Egyptian goddess Horus (who appeared in the guise of a mystical cow) and with the Hindu belief that the cow is holy. According to psychics, cows can absorb and negate evil or negative vibrations.

The cow and bull as beasts of sacrifice have known sanctification down the ages. In this respect, the Dun cow and the starry Taurean bull impart to us the spiritual message that the lower earthly self of humankind, as symbolized by their physicality, must be sacrificed. Humankind must gain mastery over the powerful, vigorous bull of its animal nature and make of it a sacrificial offering so that the vitality of its blood might be poured upon the germinating seed of the spirit, the Light Within. And so Mithras, god of the sun, physical counterpart of the spiritual sun that shines in mystery behind our star of earth, heralds the great task of the Christ and of St. George (whose day falls on April 23) coming in with the Taurean influences, following Easter with its time-honored story of crucifixion, death, and resurrection.

As will be explained, the missions of Mithras, Christ, and St. George interrelate.

 odiac

TAURUS—BULL
APRIL 20–MAY 21

ANGEL: Archangel Anael
RULING PLANET: Venus

KEYWORD: Acquisition—building, abundance, possessions, creating a receptacle in the earthly domain to contain the harmony of the spheres

AGE: Youth (14–21 years)

METAL: Copper

CROSS: Fixed (the Father)

ELEMENT: Earth

QUALITIES: Strong-willed, toiling, practical, sensuous, musical, literary, artistic, temperate, moist, fruitful, magnetic, beneficent, intractable

ILLNESSES TO GUARD AGAINST: Weakness in the throat or neck, congestion in the chest, afflictions arising from diet

BODY AREAS: Throat, neck

STONES: Sapphire, emerald, turquoise, lapis lazuli, moss agate, jade, opal

NUMBER: 6

DAY: Friday

FLOWERS AND HERBS: Lily of the valley, violet, wild and red garden rose, myrtle-blossom, coltsfoot

TREES: Almond, apple, walnut, ash, sycamore, cherry, myrtle

ANIMALS: Bull, cow

BIRDS: Dove, sparrow, swan

COLOR: All shades of blue and green, turquoise, soft rose-pinks

The name *Taurus* is associated in ancient Egypt with the season for plowing the soil with oxen, and with Mount Taurus in Asia.

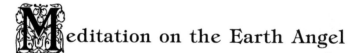editation on the Earth Angel

Light a candle, alone in your room or in some secluded place in nature, and dedicate it to the Earth Angel (safety jars should be used out of doors to avoid starting a fire). Begin to see with the eyes of inner vision the form of this great Earth Angel, one of the archangels of the four elements. See her flowing garments of blue, green, a swirling mystery of turquoise and soft earth colors; these lovely vestments that radiate from her being and play upon the earth as rays of magical splendor are the spiritual substance from which form is created by divine intelligence. Throughout the folds of these robes of light dance the fairies, the "little people" of the four elements, although some are taller than the tallest human being. The innumerable fairies and angels that work under the direction of the Earth Angel embrace all four elements, because each one harmonizes and combines its individual essence under the instruction of its own angel to create a multitude of life forms. The Earth Angel directs her throng of joyous workers, nature spirits, and angels to build form with physical matter, so that they initiate birth, death and recycling in the bodies of humankind, plants, animals, and the mineral kingdom. All is under the ministration of the radiant Earth Angel who permeates the cosmos with her shining mystic robes.

As in peace you contemplate the wonder and the miracle of this mighty angel, you might feel it is right to send forth your human love as a gift from the heart to this noble being whose very essence is giving; and, in so doing, you will draw close to the Earth Angel and the vast angelic host who have humanity in their care. As you attune yourself more deeply to this radiant company, you will surely begin to feel the love and the exquisite inspiration of the angels in your every-day life. In time, your vision will open out to the vista of their angelic world. They will open the door, because you will have sounded the right note, the password, which is human love.

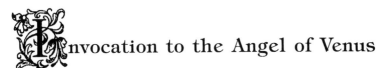 nvocation to the Angel of Venus

Use this simple prayer to ask the archangel of Venus, Anael, to bless and bring harmony to a romantic relationship. Light a candle at Anael's hour (between 9 and 10 A.M.) and burn some rose incense. Scatter a few pink rose petals on your "altar."

> Archangel Anael, angel of the mystic planet Venus, as
> I light this candle, my consciousness opens to receive
> your divine influence and the blessing of your wisdom

and loveliness. I envision you descending to meet me as I rise in thought and in spirit to reach your exalted realms. I am aware of the exquisite roselight within which you have your being and within which you enclose me as in an aura. It is as if we come together to meet in a temple of the rose.

I ask that you hear my prayer and that I may receive the benison of your assistance. Please clear the way so that the love between [insert your lover's name] and myself might blossom and flourish. Please help us to draw light from our hearts so that it may be perfectly expressed in body, mind, soul, and spirit.

Archangel Anael, you have the romantic affairs of humankind under your divine rulership, I watch this candle flame burn and behold the strength and the power of the bond of love to overcome all resentment and disharmony. I ask that you cleanse our vision of all illusion so that we may see the truth and the beauty in one another and transcend all earthly barriers and limitations.

If this petition is for all good in its conception, may it succeed. I see the archangel Anael pouring out blessings upon us as if from a horn of plenty; and these blessings merge into one brilliant shaft of light, which penetrates the heart of our love so that it may be healed and be whole.

Thank the archangel and move quietly away from your altar, allowing the candle to burn down in silence.

Stars of Spring

It is easy to find Virgo (the Virgin) with its bright star Spica ("ear of wheat"), as the constellation lies next to Leo in the skies and is the most striking star group of the springtime. It is to be seen to the left of Leo, slightly lower in the sky. It is readily identifiable, its

figure representing a capital Y turned on its side. Once it has been located, it is easy to see the hooded corn maiden within the structure of its glyph, that corn goddess who signifies the Madonna, the Virgin, and Mother Earth. Symbolically enough, that region of the sky between the open arms of the Y and the star Beta Leonis, is the point known as the galactic pole, the point in the northern sky at the greatest distance from the Milky Way; it is of this area that the astronomer Herschel noted the "remarkable purity and clearness of the heavens"; this clarity tallies well with the Virgin, especially when we consider that it is here that astronomers are able to use their instruments to penetrate far into space, beyond the boundaries of our galactic system, because of the strange and phenomenal lucidity of the heavens.

Higher than Virgo and to the left of Leo shines the constellation Coma Berenices, or "the Hair of Berenice," queen of Egypt. Queen Berenice vowed to offer her hair to the gods if they brought her husband safely home from war. Her prayers were answered, and she sheared her locks and placed them with due dedication in a temple. Shortly afterward they disappeared, the royal astronomer pronouncing that they had been accepted by the gods and, transfigured into stars, elevated to the celestial regions in honor of the Egyptian queen's faithful love.

Below Virgo and Leo are the two constellations the Crow (Corvus) and the Cup (Crater). The Crow is kite-shaped and can be identified by the trapezium formed by its four chief stars, one of which, at its northeastern corner, is a double star, the lesser of these two being the Raven. The raven is a link with Celtic mythology, as ravens were sacred as birds of wisdom bearing the secrets of the gods and of life, death, and immortality; the crow was a lesser being, associated with mischievous gods such as Mercury and Loki and the thieving hero Prometheus. The crow is less than a god (symbolized by the raven) and yet of the same family as the raven, and so a lesser being made in the image of the godhead.

The Cup is less noticeable than the Crow; however, if the Crow is humanity, it is interesting that the Cup (representative of the Grail) was placed by the intuitive Ptolemy next to the Crow and due west of him, as according to the old tales, the Celtic paradise lies in the west.

The three stars that are visible in the Cup form a triangle. It is not very distinct, and both the Crow and the Cup require the stargazer to make a patient study of the springtime skies before either is likely to be easily identified.

WISEWOMAN'S JOURNAL

Cuckoo Spells for Dreaming, Love, and Destiny

If, in the days of spring, you should hear the cuckoo call in the early hours,* after midnight when it is still pitch dark, you may know your future thus: if the moon by which it calls is new, that means happiness in love; if it is waxing, that means a new love; if it is full, that means marriage; if it is waning, that means a long engagement. But if you should hear the midnight cuckoo in the dark of the moon, which is the time of the Morrigan, then beware, for it means your lover boils with dark passions and is full of terrible secrets.

Count the cuckoo's notes when you first hear them in the spring; as is their number, so do they indicate the number of years that must pass before a maiden is to be married; and if there are very many, the divining maid need not despair, for in that case she must count them as months. If you have foreknowledge of your wedding day, the spell will not work. If you are to

*There is an ancient fable according to which the cuckoo and the dove are the two birds that are admitted to heaven.

live and die in single blessedness, the cuckoo will bring to you a dream; and in that dream an angel or a spirit or yet a figure that is the semblance of the goddess will offer you a gown of white silk, which you will put on. It is a sign of honor, and indicates to your heart that there is some divine purpose to your single state.

The cuckoo is a fairy bird and sings in time to the heartbeat of the earth. She is herald of the spring and ushers in its spirit. She is a bird of the goddess, and as she brings the bounty of the springtime, so must her blessings also demand their proper sacrifice; and so her progeny are laid as gifts in other birds' nests, which then hatch and dispossess the young of those birds of their home and their parents, so that they die on the ground beneath the nest. Old wives who know in their souls that the cuckoo is a bird of the goddess say that she turns into a hawk in winter, for their wisdom tells them that the goddess is the giver and the taker of life. When she gives life, she is the cuckoo of the spring and the early summer. When she takes life, she is a hawk of the grim winter. Old wives say too that her spirit enters into the underground fairy halls to pass the winter, although her creature form flies to the summerlands.

Omens

Good luck is with you if you hear the cuckoo call on April 28. If you first hear her soft notes on April 6, she warns you to be cautious in your endeavors. If you hear her calling to your right, she sings to you that all is well; to your left, she urges you to beware. If at that time you are walking on lush grass or the fragrant soil of a woodland, that is good; but if you stand on harsh, stony, barren ground, or on the surface of a lane or a road You must say:

> Cuckoo spirit, fly hither,
> Chase evil luck thither.

If you have money in your pocket when you hear the cuckoo call (and especially should that be the first time in the year), turn it over at once and speak this charm:

Lucky coins, now I count thee,
Cuckoo-fairy bring me bounty.

Then, while you are still fingering the coins, make a wish, and it is bound to come true.

When the cuckoo brings you good tidings, they last the year round; when she gives warning, you must look sharp for the next twelve months.

When the cuckoo calls through the woods bright and early in the spring, a lovely long warm summer is forecast; and if the cuckoo should call more than twenty-one times all at once, that is a sure sign of coming rain, warm and genial, showering upon the earth to bring forth the flowers and pretty grasses of spring and to coax the buds to burst on the trees.

Author's Note

Reference to the "midnight cuckoo" might cause some confusion—in fact, on fine spring nights it has been known for the cuckoo to call through the dark, past midnight, and on into the early hours. In Britain the cuckoo has always been regarded as a sacred bird;* its Celtic connections are suggested by its name in Cheshire of the Welsh ambassador, and in Cornwall (once a country in its own right with a significant Celtic history) the Cuckoo Feast on the Sunday nearest April 28 still commemorates the day on which this magical bird is supposed to usher in the spring. The story goes that one evening in April, when the weather was bitterly cold as if it were still the depths of winter, a farmer invited some friends to share his hearth, throwing a great hollow log upon the fire to keep it blazing for their comfort. A cuckoo flew out of the hollow log, and, from that moment, the weather altered, turning warm and bringing in the soft airs of spring.

The cuckoo is associated with country fairs across Britain,

*North-country people often declared the day a holiday when they first heard the cuckoo.

especially in Sussex, where the Old Woman who has guardianship over all the cuckoos and lets them out at Heathfield Fair on April 14 suggests associations with the goddess. This Old Woman, who controls the seasons, releases cuckoos in plenty if she is in an amiable mood, but only a few if human beings have raised her anger; she thereby confers her blessings either abundantly or frugally. Ceridwen, the mother goddess of the Celts, dispensing the sacred Awen—the waters of life and death—from her mystic cauldron, seems to be implicated here.

The Easter Hare Spell

As the cuckoo is the bird of spring, so the hare is the creature sacred to the springtime. The Easter hare spell is best essayed by the light of the full moon of March or April. As soon as the evening light has all but stolen away, you must make your way to the edge of a field or a meadow (or if you are a town dweller, you may sit alone in your room and contemplate the picture of such in your mind) and so that you may have good health all the year round and cast off any ailments that afflict you, speak this rune aloud to the hares that live in secret and run by night thereabouts:

> Hare spirit, swift as lightning
> The devils in me need affrighting
> Brightest angels in high heaven
> Fright them from me seventy-times-seven
> Now do they reside in you
> Run, run, hare spirit, till fall of dew.

This is not to curse the hares with your maladies to make them sick, but to translate them to the hares so that they may carry them off for you and so purify them.

When you have done, hurry home and light a white candle on the cusp of Raphael's hour, which is one hour before midnight. Draw a hare on virgin paper and inscribe it with those afflictions you wish to be rid of. Then burn it up in the candle flame, repeating the rune as given. Give thanks to Raphael and to the hare spirit and light a bowl of incense to burn along side your candle. Now meditate upon the swift and graceful hare and let your soul take flight. Pass it into the hare and let it run free and fleet in the form of the hare; let your soul run wild and unfettered over the wide meadows and upon the open hillsides as often as you feel nervous or full of frustration and weariness, and you will keep your spirits sparkling and childlike as if they lived in an eternal springtide. Do not forget this teaching, for it is an old trick of the witches.

Author's Note

The hare is sacred to the Anglo-Saxon goddess Eastre ("goddess of the east"), who is associated with spring, because the season suggests the sun rising in the east, the bright new morning of the year after the darkness of winter. As sacrifice and renewal is an eternal Eastertide theme, both the cuckoo and the hare embrace those ideas, the cuckoo as already described and the unfortunate hare by being the victim of the reprehensible sport of hare-coursing. The Easter hare lays the Easter eggs that are still traditional today. This country lore echoes Britain's druidic past when the egg was a sacred emblem to the priesthood; it signified the directive principle enshrined in matter and about to express its form by means of the creative principle. These sacred eggs were called "serpents' eggs."

The moon, mistress of matter, is implicated here, and so it seems appropriate that Easter as a festival is regulated by the paschal moon, the first full moon between the vernal equinox (that time of the year when daylight and nighttime hours are of equal length) and fourteen days afterward; therefore, Easter Sunday falls between March 21 and April 25. It is of note that, whether Easter falls when the sun is passing through Aries or in Taurus, both are represented by sacrificial animals (the ram and the bull), so, in each case, the symbolism is faithful to the Easter theme. April used to be called Ostermonath—the month of the Ost-end wind or wind from the east—and Easter was the old April Feast, which lasted for eight days (even in pre-Christian times giving intimations of the Resurrection). The sun was believed to dance on Easter day,* and so the sun and the moon are brought into play through the agency of myth and story, the mother and the father eternally courting to create the world anew in spring through the divine principle of love—the child of both.

A Dreaming Spell for St. George's Day

Upon St. George's Eve (that being the twenty-second day of April, as the saint's memorial day falls on the twenty-third of the month) be sure to take to bed with you some slips of paper and a pen, setting them at your bedside, for it is good on this holy night of the year to perform a dreaming spell in the old way, as idle dreams you dream this night will bear for you a message that must be divined and borne in mind as a spiritual key for the rest of the year.

Fast for three hours before retiring. Make up a tisane of one part mugwort, one part rue, and two parts loosestrife. This is a witch's brew and will bring to you that quality of calm and restfulness in sleep that is needed to work the spell. Now you

---

* Visions of the sun dancing and spinning are recorded in connection with Our Lady of Fatima, who gave three secrets to three Italian country children, one of which the Vatican has decided not to reveal.

must light a white or a silver candle and prepare a ritual bath, which is done by adding sea salt, valerian, and henbane to the running water, a pinch of each;* and be sure to ask the blessings of the angel Asariel as you pour it. Bathe in these sacred waters by the single light of the silver candle and repeat thrice this charm:

> Mother Moon, smile on my dreams
> Bring their true message on thy soft beams.

Think awhile upon the solemnity of your purpose, and when you have finished bathing, dress in fresh clean night attire and arrange your bed with snowy white linen all clean and fresh likewise, taking care to place three sprigs of rosemary beneath your pillow.

Take a wineglass of the witch's tea to bed with you and imbibe it slowly in little sips. As you do so, you must call the bird of your soul forth and let it fly in fancy three times around the room, so that it may soar free as soon as you fall into slumber.

Now speak this prayer in all reverence to the angel who will reveal celestial wisdom to you in your dreams:

> Noble Iachadiel, bless this mystic dreaming spell
> Bring pure counsel to my soul
> The mystery of its visions unfold.

And whenever you awake, either throughout the night or in the morning, write down every sound that you hear, each thing

* Henbane is a toxic herb and should not be taken internally except under the guidance of a qualified herbalist.

that you see, every feeling that passes over your soul, and every thought that you think while you are in dreamland, or while you hover between its shores and the edge of wakefulness. Keep these notes and meditate upon them often in the coming days.

Author's Note

This spell seems to be especially appropriate for Easter, as it was during the Passion that Christ entered the Underworld to learn its secrets before rising again on the third day. It is also given with due respect to St. George as the patron or guiding saint for England, although, as it is believed that St. George is also associated with the great spirit Ar-Thor, guardian spirit of the British Isles, it might be inappropriate to limit him to the frontiers of England. We might suppose that St. George has guardianship over all Britain. He is, in any case, also associated with the Aragon, Portugal, and the Holy Land.

Few facts have come down to us concerning St. George. We know that he was martyred at Lydda, Palestine, possibly for refusing to burn incense to the Roman emperor and so accept him as a god. His struggle with a dragon is mentioned in the Golden Legend, which claims that, having successfully slain the dragon, he put off his knightly habit, gave all he had to the poor, and set forth to enlighten others in the precepts of Christianity. He was martyred in 287 and first became recognized as England's patron saint under the Norman kings.

Uccello, painting in the dawn of the Renaissance, portrayed St. George fulfilling his task. With his lance, St. George has pierced the dragon's eye. To his left stands the archetypal Virgin or maiden, to whom the dragon is chained. In the sky among the clouds, above the lance of St. George, is the eye of God. (The painting is in the National Gallery in London.)

The dragon in its essence might be looked upon as an ideograph for the lower nature of humanity, which clings to the little isolated ego of selfhood and can see no farther than promoting the interests of itself. And, yet, it would surely be a mistake to look upon the dragon as purely symbolic of "evil." In mythology, the dragon guards hidden treasure. It breathes fire, yet, as the Chinese rain-dragon, it can also bring the nourishment of rain. The Roman dragon was a benign creature, sacred to the mother goddess of nature and the harvest. The red dragon, emblem of Wales, echoes the emblem of Uther Pendragon, father of King Arthur; the fact that he ordered two golden dragons to be made may give a clue to the duality inherent in the nature of the dragon. The dragon has to be slain by St. George, yet the dragon also has connections with the engendering of the guardian spirit of Britain whose earthly counterpart is King Arthur. In ancient Greece the dragon was endowed with the gift of prophecy and was a keeper of the sacred secrets of the earth. In Teutonic mythology, the evil and cunning serpent Nidhogg lies curled around the divine Tree of Life, its tail in its mouth, eternally gnawing at the tree roots; yet Friedrich Kekulé was visited in a dream by this creature, so enabling him to discover the pattern of the benzene ring, the atomic structure of the benzene molecule, which empowered him to benefit humanity.

In his book *Into the New Age,* Stephen Verney links the task of St. George with that of the Christ in whose name St. George slays the dragon. The serpent of the lower self is not in itself intrinsically evil but has become so because it masquerades as our master when its true function is to serve. It has to be "slain," that is, it has to be pierced with the light of god-consciousness, the lance of our higher or spiritual self, that which is a flicker of light of the godhead. And so, in Uccello's painting, the eye of God, the lance of St. George, and the eye of the dragon become one, a flow of divine consciousness from above to below, with the lance as the sacred conductor of divine energy. St. George's true mission is revealed. He is not to slay the dragon but to tame or transfigure it. The old myths identify the dragon essence: the Egyptian god of the sun, Ra, conquers Apophis, the dragon of all darkness; the Buddha touches the heart of a deadly dragon to transform it into the guardian of the truth, a creature who cradles in its protective claws the pearl of wisdom. Grace Cooke, one of the great seers of our age, affirms in her book *The Light in Britain*, that the Uffington White Horse is actually a dragon, lying slain upon the hill as a symbol; and yet it is white in its "death," signifying renewal, purity, and identifying with the unicorn, which symbolizes sublime intelligence transfigured into enlightenment and spiritual perception by means of its third eye or horn. This horn, from another aspect, is St. George's lance.

Turning again to Uccello's painting, it seems only right that the dragon's features are illuminated by gentleness and wisdom, which shine forth from the wound that is the cause of its terrible suffering. The hide of the selfish ego dwelling in the darkness of materialism is thick, and penetration is agony for a moment; yet penetration is also mercy, because the dragon is a beast that breathes fire and swallows its tail, and so the withholding of the blow of quickened consciousness would be to allow it utterly to consume and destroy itself. Yet, of itself, it is beloved, for when it is pierced, the dragon offers up the treasure it guards. It becomes itself the treasure—the servant, the perfect receptacle for spirit—the precious Cup personified which is the Holy Grail.

Perhaps this was the true mission of Christ—the revelation to humanity, through the cosmic drama he enacted, that each soul must pierce and transform the dragon of his or her lower self, so that the light of the spirit might flood in and subsume the rage and terror of the beast, transforming it into the kindly creature of wisdom we see in Uccello's painting. So the dark age of Kali, the age of materialism, might be overcome, for in the old story the maiden leads the tamed dragon through the marketplace—a symbol, perhaps, of a selfish and greedy soul-environment that can no longer tempt the dragon or raise in him again the fires of oppression, ruthlessness, and self-seeking that lead to inevitable self-swallowing. And so Mithras slays the bull, and his blood pours out upon the earth and is the source of renewal, of rebirth for that subterranean dimension.

Yet, as indicated by legend and Uccello's painting, the Virgin, the maiden, the woman, shares a special relationship with the dragon. She is chained to him, and he to her. She is an especial victim of the age of dark materialism, because she is, in her own being, the bearer of fruit, of progeny, and is linked to the earth goddess herself. She suffers, like the planet, from the affliction of rape and domination. Yet her very chains are also the symbol of her freedom, because it is she who leads the dragon through the marketplace. The chain that oppressed her has newly become the chain that declares that the dragon has been tamed and transformed. Moreover, she is the inspiration, the guiding light that urged St. George on to dare to fulfill his task. When it is done, she is freed from the morbid imbalance that expressed itself through the principle of materialism.

It is, surely, humanity as a whole that must "slay" the dragon; but perhaps woman has a special role as teacher and purveyor of the wisdom that forms St. George's lance. It is the maiden who leads the dragon through the marketplace, and Mary Magdalen who first recognized the arisen Christ walking in the garden on Easter morning.

WISEWOMAN'S WEATHERBOOK

When the sheep in the meadows nestle at peace on the grass together with their lambkins, or graze quietly, expect the weather to stay as meek and mild as they are; but when they shift and roam restlessly, and bleat and baa loudly to one another, and are full of nervous unease and indisposition, heavy soaking rain will soon be falling, and a thunderstorm with high winds may be on its way.

❧

Look to the Evening Star, which is Venus, in the summer months; if it rides low in the heavens with the leader star of the Bear's tail sharp and glittering like a banner over it, there will be only feeble life in that year's summer, and the crops will not be abundant or vigorous; but if the beautiful Evening Star is to be seen together with the moon while the daylight sky still glows blue before the fall of dusk, that tranquil sight may reassure you, for the maleficent aspect will be weakened.

❧

In the summertime when the swallows swoop near the ground, you can be sure the weather will soon be as mardy* as a soaked cat.

❧

Watch the morning mists on a summer's day; if they float up into the sky like a flock of white doves, the day will be fair and long-lived; but if they sink to the ground and creep and skulk away into the ditches, it will be a wet and dreary day, and darkness will fall early.

---

* *Mardy* is an old Yorkshire word that means petulant, fitful, or miserable.

Chapter Three

MAY

Beltane, Ring of Fire

Sister, Awake

Sister, awake! Close not your eyes!
The day her light discloses
And the bright morning doth arise
Out of her bed of roses.

Therefore awake! Make haste, I say,
And let us, without staying,
All in our gowns of green so gay
Into the Park a-maying!

British folksong

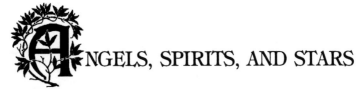

NGELS, SPIRITS, AND STARS

Echoing St. George and his struggle with the dragon, the Geminian constellation, twinkling clear and sharp in the winter skies,* suggests to the student of symbols the power and wisdom of the serpent, for the emblem of the Star Twins is the famous serpent-entwined caduceus.

*Winter is the season when Gemini can be delineated most clearly in the heavens.

The caduceus was given to Mercury, herald of the gods. The angel of the planet Mercury is Raphael, angel of healing. In mythology he is often identified with Merlin, wizard-guardian of King Arthur; so although Mercury, reflecting the qualities of his element quicksilver, is an elusive, laughing, mischievous god, full of trickery and practical jokes like his Teutonic counterpart, Loki, and the Greek hero-god Prometheus, who stole the divine fire from Mount Olympus for humanity only to be horribly punished for his pains, he is also the god of healing and compassion. Mercury is a winged god, and his caduceus is also depicted as winged. In his book *The Migration of Symbols*, written in 1894, Count Goblet D'Alviella describes how this ancient emblem blends with the trisula, which corresponds to the winged globe, the scarab, the lotus, the lingam, and the tree of Buddha. The progenitive powers of the sacred serpent are suggested by the association of the caduceus with the scarab and the lingam, and the special role of the serpent as keeper of divine truths is indicated by the interchangeability of the caduceus with the winged globe, the trisula, the lotus, and the tree of Buddha—all of which signify wisdom.

Homer describes the caduceus as a wand entwined with the figures of two serpents embracing, one male, one female. To the Romans it was a white wand which their officers carried when they went to treat for peace. This theme is repeated in Milton's *Paradise Lost* when the poet refers to it as an "opiate rod" by which Hermes (Mercury)

> drove in silent shoals the lingering train
> To Night's dull shore and Pluto's dreary reign.

Mercury was able to dispense sleep with his caduceus; from its dual symbolism, as giver of sleep to soothe and heal and as that agency in the human psyche that shuts down vision, the starry twins are indicated.

The Geminian twins are, of course, Castor and Pollux, the two brightest stars in the constellation.* Castor is the mortal, earthly brother of Pollux, the twin who represents the immortal spirit dwelling in heavenly bliss with the supreme godhead, the golden and divine

* *Castor* means "tamer of horses;" *Pollux* means "the pugilist."

reflection of Castor, his wellspring of hope and vision. Like the Christed Nazarene who would not enter Paradise without first sharing the karma of erring humanity, or the Buddha, who, just about to leave the earth plane for the realms of Nirvana, spied a gnat being snapped up by a bat and decided to remain in service to the earth until all its creatures were released from the great wheel of death and rebirth, Pollux will not, perhaps cannot, attain to Elysium until Castor too awakes from the sleep of earth or materialism and becomes one with Pollux, his heavenly reflection. So Pollux dispenses healing, and yet Castor sleeps. The serpents that twist around the wand are not yet reconciled. It is perhaps apposite to note here that the caduceus is the time-honored emblem of the medical profession in England and the United States; with its power to heal, and the state of sleep it reveals in its orthodox attitude to holistic medicine and therapies, an irony is revealed; such immemorial symbols speak a deeper truth than that which we would consciously choose to express.

What is the essence of our sleep of mortality, and how shall we awaken from it? Mercury, god and spirit, provides a clue. He is of the mind, of quicksilver thought, the ghost in the intellect who gives lightning flashes of insight and inspiration. In one sense he is divine intelligence, discriminating, analyzing, linking spirit, psyche, and body with the brilliance and purity of his mind-essence. On the higher mental planes, Mercury is eternally dancing. We need his agility to develop our consciousness; we need his glittering efficiency to set in motion the line of communication between the sublime spheres of exalted spirit and our sublunary environment, dark as it is down here on earth and in need of the quickening influence of the silver of the moon.* But as has been said of alcohol, Mercury is a bridge, not a way.

In our age of Aquarius there is a particular danger that, in our present state of development, we may champion the intellect to a degree that far outweighs its actual significance. Believing that the rational, analytical intellect is all, we become entrapped in a strange gray world of suffocating limitation, inhabited by all kinds of unpleasant demons and phantoms of illusion. This has already happened in the

* The marriage of the sun and the moon is believed to represent, in esoteric terms, the wedding of the mind (moon) with the spirit (sun).

spheres of organized thought that dominate our times, and accounts for the hopeless inability to understand humanity's true need.

Mercury is nothing if not subtle, and his unbalanced influence can lead us astray even as we seek to avoid the snares he sets for us. A huge and revitalizing wave of spiritual resurgence is challenging the world of gray mental concepts that has been sucking dry the lifelines of communion with the inner planes of consciousness, the source of true life. These very lines of communication come under Mercurial influences, and there is a danger that, instead of making a strong and sound soul-connection with the refined worlds within, Mercury may play us a trick and set us wandering aimlessly in a trackless wilderness where there is a bewildering burgeoning of information about the approach to the spirit on the mental plane, but no true nourishment for the soul as the processes of intellectualization cause it to starve.

It is said that there is a doorway to hell at the gates of heaven, just as there is a doorway to heaven at the gates of hell. The brain, in common with the rest of the body, can be overindulged and blind us to the inner verities. Before we can wholly respond to the fine and quickening influences of Mercury and Venus, the morning and evening stars, there is a need to encounter and overcome those inner areas of confusion and ignorance that respond negatively to their inspiration.

Once awareness begins to develop into the recognition that Mercury's duality is a beautiful growth toward oneness, the *wisdom* of the serpent (also a symbol of rampant unharmonized sexual power) begins gently to exert and assert itself. Then we may begin to obey Christ's exhortation to be "as wise as serpents and as innocent as doves" (the latter being sacred to Venus) so that the great heresy of separation, of alienation and strife-torn duality, might be overcome and our souls healed in their innermost depths. This is the true mission of Mercury as healer and planet closest to the sun. Physically, the orb of Mercury is small and swift, its speed excelling that of earth by almost four times. It can be seen as dawn breaks in the east, and in the west, as the sun sets, depending on the time of year. Considering Mercury's esoteric dual nature, it is not surprising to learn from astronomical calculations that it is a planet of extremes, of intense heat and intense cold always in coexistence. A single rotation on its axis and a single revolution of the sun are the same measurement of time for Mercury, exposing its globe to perpetual blazing summer on one side and deepest deathly winter of eternal night and cold on the other (these conditions are similar to the moon in relation to the earth and link Mercury's silvery reflective aspect to hers). It is surely the way we choose to reflect Mercury's qualities and gifts that determines whether Hermes will lead us to the "dark regions of the imprisoned dead" and drive us to "Night's dull shore and Pluto's dreary reign" (Pluto is the planet farthest from the sun, almost lost in dark space beyond Neptune, the mythological symbol of death and the Underworld), which symbolize the sleep of the mind entombed in materialism, or inspire us in triumph to follow the sun, as Mercury does on the physical and inner planes.

Mythology makes Mercury the original creator of the lyre. He presides over music, art, science, magic, meditation and reflection, prudence, cunning, and theft. He steals the spiritual sunlight for humanity's exaltation and yet suffers for it. It is interesting that Prometheus, Mercury's prototype, who steals the god-fire from Mount Olympus in Greek legend, is punished by a terrible eagle who strips his flesh and claws out his liver daily, the hapless Prometheus being bound to a rockface to facilitate his penance, his life restored to him each night so that his suffering might be endlessly perpetuated. The eagle, in myth, is a spiritual messenger (like Mercury himself) and is endowed with the mystical quality of being able to gaze unflinchingly into the heart of the sun. In its entirety, the picture seems to suggest that the gift of the flame of pure spirit is dearly bought and can be realized only by the pain and suffering inherent in sacrificing the lower self. The invention of astronomy, the musical scale, weights and measures, boxing and gymnastics, dance and drama, are attributed to Mercury. He is the god of peaceful commerce, of enlightened communication in barter, and of friendship.

A beautiful tale of Mercurial significance is told of Rubi, a member of the Cherubim, or "Spirits of Knowledge," who was with Eve when she walked in Paradise. He had great reverence for her and took one of her daughters under his especial care and instruction. The girl's name was Liris, youthful and intellectually vigorous, eager for knowledge and cerebral satisfaction, and proud and ruthless in her quest for it. Rubi (Raphael?) fell in love with her and, at her request, revealed his radiant form to her eyes.

Liris immediately embraced him (a symbol of humankind's egotistical tendency to wish to possess the supreme knowledge, powers, and gifts of the spiritual spheres) and was burnt to ashes in a moment by the intensity of the light that flowed forth from Rubi. Where her kiss had touched his brow he felt forever afterward a burning brand of agony that knew no abatement, its impress destined to be stamped there for all time.

This story, given in Sir Thomas More's *Loves of the Angels*, may have the same origin as the Prometheus legend; in this version of the myth, Mercury's special connection with humanity is emphasized; he is often depicted as half-god, half-mortal (as Castor and Pollux bear out). This conception of humanity is perhaps a true one, for Mercury and his element quicksilver represent the silvered cosmic mirror through which humanity gazes to perceive its real reflection as half mortal and half divine, and through which it must step so that the illusion and "glamour" of the earth-plane is finally overcome, along with the terrible suffering that this duality brings. Mercury steals light or enlightenment for humanity, but must pay the cost of wielding such a double-edged sword, for that same enlightenment can be sullied by the desires of the ego and become an *ignis fatuus*, a false light whose lurid attraction threatens to become the source of destruction.

The fable of Liris and her angel remains an instructive one in the deepest sense.

odiac

GEMINI—TWINS
MAY 22–JUNE 20

ANGEL: Archangel Raphael
RULING PLANET: Mercury
KEYWORD: Communication—attributes of the higher and lower mental bodies—vital intelligence and inspirational wisdom, reflection, discrimination
AGE: Girlhood, boyhood (7–14 years)
METAL: Mercury (quicksilver)
CROSS: Mutable
ELEMENT: Air

QUALITIES: Communicative, inventive, alert, inquisitive, swift, sharp, versatile, dry, mental, ardent, youthful, mobile, idealistic

ILLNESSES TO GUARD AGAINST: Afflictions of the shoulders, lungs and chest; biliousness, nervous debility, nervous diseases

BODY AREAS: Shoulders, chest, lungs

STONES: Diamond, jade, chrysoprase, agate, aquamarine, topaz

NUMBER: 5

DAY: Wednesday

FLOWERS AND HERBS: Parsley, dill, hazel, snapdragon, fern, iris

TREES: Elder, filbert

ANIMALS: Dog, squirrel, serpent

BIRDS: Parrot, linnet, eagle, finches

COLOR: White, silver, yellow, spring green, pale gray

The name *Gemini* is from the Latin *geminus* for "twin," indicating Castor and Pollux, the two bright stars in the Gemini constellation.

nvocation to Raphael and the Healing Angels

Light a white or a gold candle at Raphael's hours (7 A.M., 3 P.M., 11 P.M.) and create an aura around yourself of stillness and peace. Begin to perceive the folds of the angel Raphael's garment as it opens to receive you into a healing temple of perfect sanctuary, kindliness, and love. You may like to think of the angel Raphael as a mother figure enrobed in soft blues of gentle cerulean and deep Madonna hues, with golden hands shining like sunlight, which will be placed upon you to bestow blessing and compassion and the warmth of healing love.

Study the candle flame as it aspires to a golden point of prayer, and say these words:

> Angel Raphael and the host of healing angels, brothers of the flame, I pray that you may direct the healing

forces to me so that I may receive them harmoniously and reverently.* I watch the golden candle flame burning and enter into peace and stillness. I blend my deeper being with the flame so that I become one with the sun's glory. I see the sun shining in my heart and shedding its radiant beauty throughout my body, mind, and soul so that every shadow is chased away and all darkness is transformed into a golden stream of pulsating light, vibrant with joy and vitality and healing, the very stuff of life itself. In triumph and gladness I receive the divine draft of healing. Giving thanks from my innermost self, I affirm I am healed, I am healed, I am healed.

Breathe gently and steadily and allow the healing hands of the angels to hold you in light as the candle burns down.

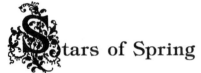

Stars of Spring

The Hunting Dogs (or Canes Venatici) shine on spring nights below the Plough and above Virgo and Leo. The brightest star in the constellation, Charles's Heart (Cor Caroli), was said to have sparkled with preternatural brilliance on the eve of Charles II's entry into London for the first time after the Restoration, presumably in celebration of the healing of a national split between the Roundheads and the Cavaliers. The name "Hunting Dogs" seems also to have royal connotations, as the "sport" of hunting (both Satan and God are often personified as hounds of darkness or light in myth and poetry) was initially a royal prerogative.

Hydra (the "water snake") is the longest constellation of the firmament. It winds from Libra to the borders of Cancer, and may be located by its northernmost stars, which mark the head of the water snake. The most significant star of the constellation is Alpha Hydrae, or Al Fard,

---

*Name any part of your body in need of healing (if your illness is not physical, say "my mental body, emotional body, center of nervous energy," etc.).

the "solitary one." Al Fard has a reddish hue and was known to the ancient Chinese astronomers as the "red bird."

Directly above the head of the Hydra monster, between Gemini and Leo, the Crab (Cancer) appears in the springtime skies. It has eight stars, which frame the faint and mysterious cluster known as the Beehive (Praesepe), visible to the naked eye as a dim cloud. The ancients noted this and, unaware of its striking characteristics when viewed through a telescope, classified it as a "nebula," the first time this term was used to denote celestial phenomena. The esoteric ideas that apply to Cancer are also linked to the Beehive.

 ISEWOMAN'S JOURNAL

The Domino Lovespell

When a young maid wishes to fulfill the quest of augury, then she must wait for the time of the waxing moon in May, which belongs to Diana the Huntress. Let her find a room that catches its beams, and should the air without be soft and springlike, it is well to throw open the window of the chamber onto the shadows of the night and the moon's shine.

She should play a sacred game of dominoes by the strong white rays of Diana's moon and by the light of a single green candle, lit at Raphael's hour, which is the hour before midnight. She should have by her side a basket of good strong wicker, its interior to be strewn with unblemished rose leaves, and she should empty the full set of dominoes into it so that their faces are unseen, all the while silently repeating her prayer that she might be granted the wisdom to gaze through futurity's casement onto the changing seas of her fate. Let her be aware of her quest, and of its magic, for Diana's moon is above her.

Now she may draw a domino at random. If it should be a double number, the stars are smiling on her. If the number be even, there is a whisper in the night telling of star-crossed lovers; a double six shows a speedy fulfillment of her heart's deepest wish; a double blank forbodes the desertion or falsehood of the one best beloved by her; and an odd and even number together is an omen of light and shadow, bringing in its wake compensations upon which it is the wise soul's delight to philosophize.

If the maiden draws an odd number, she may expect a sudden change in her fortunes where she would least have predicted it.

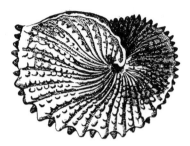

A worker of this spell must calculate the number of spots on the domino drawn and take their total as designating either an odd number or an even for the purposes of their divination. A single domino may yield more than one prediction. By way of example, if you should draw a double, then of course that must be an even number, so you must consider a second prognostication as well as that given for doubles, and blend the two oracles. Again, if for example you should draw five-two, that is odd and even together, and the digits naturally add up to produce an odd number; and so the final prognostic given, as well as the fifth, must be taken into account.

Young maidens who essay this May spell may try it three times, reshuffling the dominoes each time before drawing another. They should find that the domino oracle repeats itself in at least one instance, which means that they are working the spell as they should. If they happen to draw two doubles one after the other, that is a happy sign, indeed; but it indicates that thereafter the lips of destiny are sealed, and no more must be asked of divination that night, but that the third try should be forgone, the casement shut up, the candle extinguished, and the maid go straight to her bed, where she will dream sweet and invigorating dreams, such as only May can bring.

Author's Note

This spell seems to have a connection with May Molloch, the Celtic fairy who is associated with the May goddess through her ability to prophesy and her bestowal of the gift of fecundity to women (later perverted into a habit of child stealing when May became "Meg of the hairy arms" who stole babies from their cradles). In her original form as May she had abundant nut-brown hair, hair being symbolic of burgeoning fertility; this characteristic was translated by unsympathetic Christian superstition to her arms, and tales were told of "terrible hairy arms" reaching down the chimney to snatch infants—apparently with the intent to eat them or ensnare them in fairyland. May Molloch was originally benign and would assist in games of dominoes, draughts, and chess, using them as agents for her prophesying qualities. She also brought women dreams, perhaps of a sexual or romantic nature, which she touched with mysticism and the knowledge of the seeress. It is unclear whether the last line of the Domino Lovespell refers to May the month or May the fairy—perhaps the distinction in any case is too small to be important.

According to Virgil, the calends (first day) of May were spent by the young people of Rome in the woods and meadows, dancing and singing in honor of Flora, goddess of fruits and flowers. Flora is associated with Bona Dea, the "Good Goddess," whose magical familiars were the kindly dragons of wisdom discussed in chapter 2. Lemuralia, the Feasts of the Dead, were also celebrated in May, perhaps because this delightful month, with its manifestation of the earth-mother goddess in its springing verdure, and its approach to the summer solstice, which celebrates the godly influences, suggested the forerunners of the human race, which are said to have been the Lemurians, a dwarflike people who lived a purely emotional and instinctive life, in that the emotional body of humankind was then being formed and developed. In our present age, it is thought that we are developing the lower mental body and that the process is now complete, so that, as the Aquarian Age progresses, we will be able to leave its uncomfortable and alienating limitations behind and advance into higher emotional and mental bodies that will begin to comprehend the spiritual realms and the golden heritage of the soul.

Possibly because of these primordial stirrings and the association of May with the negative, watery, moonlike Lemurians, it is considered an unfortunate month in which to marry ("marry in May, rue the day"), although if the undertow of these currents can be brought under the harmonizing control of the spirit, the wedding of the god and the goddess, which takes place in May, confers benediction and felicity to the inauguration of romantic partnerships. The May Jewels (the Beltane bonfires) and the May Flowers were all part of this magical inner ceremony, the "wedding" being the blessed transcendence of duality; the strange, sweet scent of the may blossom, as it perfumes the beautiful evenings of this month, suggests the mystical essence of the goddess.

Maia is the mother of Mercury in Greek mythology (and so the mother of healing and magic), but the name of the month seems to derive from the Latin root *mag* (in Sanskrit, *mah*), which denotes growing and shooting, so perhaps Maia herself was named from the ancient language. *Ma* in all its many forms seems to be an eternal mantra for womanhood and motherhood, and the May goddess has her reflection in Venus, for her mystic girdle was sometimes represented as being made of flowers. The dogma and convention of organized philosophy soon began to associate the burgeoning "ma" forces with guilt, sin, and corruption, and also with the need systematically to dominate and oppress women because of their dangerous powers. So it was decreed in ancient Greece that prostitutes should wear flowered robes to identify themselves in deference to virtuous women, who were required to wear plain garments.

As the Romans celebrated the calends of May, so did the ancient Britons, erecting Maypoles; dancing in honor of Robin Hood and Maid Marian to whom May Day was consecrated; and feasting and reveling at the May games, where Morris dancing, archery, and other pastimes were riotously indulged in. A May queen was elected, and the strange figure of Jack-in-the-Green led the dances. The May queen, Maid Marian, Robin Hood and Jack-in-the-Green are all earthly representatives of the god and the goddess who are, of course, universal deities; Maid Marian and Robin Hood are also guardian spirits of Britain.

The original Maypole was the thorn that bears the may blossom, emblem of the goddess at her most secret and occult. Seemingly associated with the short season in May, prior to the blooming of the may blossom, is the "blackthorn winter," which falls between the eleventh and fourteenth days of May and is sacred to the "Ice Saints" or "Frost Saints," St. Mamertus, St. Pancratius, St. Servatius and St. Boniface. This "winter," which occurs just as the blackthorn is breaking into blossom, echoes the Celtic idea of the death of the May king, who is reborn in the summer. This short season of death and rebirth, occurring when the blossoms fall in the spring and certain plants die away (emphasized by the cuckoo who changes the notes of her song after May), suggests again the symbolism of Mercury, who brings the fire of the spring but yet must suffer sacrifice and death before his "fire" can attain its full summer glory and culminate in the autumnal fruits of wisdom. This fire may have been celebrated in the old Celtic custom of lighting the great Beltane fires on May Day, an indication of sun worship, in the deepest sense, by which the sacred flame of the spirit is adored as the secret behind the physical sun. The Celts were a deeply mystical race, and Robin Hood, who lived in the holy oak tree, has a druidical origin. When King Arthur was entrusted with the profound occult mystery that proclaimed that "the king and the land are one," Robin Hood was born in his heart and came into manifestation as an aspect of the great guardian spirit of the British Isles, Ar-Thor, whose light shines through the legends of both King Arthur and Robin.

Robin Hood is the dancing, eternally young spirit of the British countryside, enshrining all the vigor and spiritual secrets of nature. He is the Mercurial aspect of Arthur, boyish, swift, quickly invisible, puckish, full of mischief and tricks.* Prometheus-like, he steals—but, of course, only to benefit humanity and he pays the price by falling sacrificial victim to his foe, the worldly and materialistic Sheriff of Nottingham, the antithesis of nature and the goodness of the goddess and the god. But Robin Hood was born again. His wounds only had the power to administer a temporary illusion of death, because Robin is part of the British group-soul and triumphantly lives on in the minds and hearts of the people.

To commemorate Robin and his consort Maid Marian, the final selections of May from the Wisewoman's Journal have been made in their honor:

Robin Hood's Draught of Immortality

Gather upon the sixth day of the waning of the moon a handful of mistletoe leaves, the same of the fresh tender leaves of the oak, and three of last year's acorns (if you have no store, you may proceed without them). Add to these the leaves and flowers (a handful again) of the lily-of-the-valley and ten parsley

---

*In his fairy guise, he becomes Robin Goodfellow, who helps the poor with their labors.

stems, freshly picked. Put all into one pint of pure white wine, and add aniseed and two tablespoons of the best cider vinegar. Simmer for ten minutes, keeping the fire low and steady in its burning. Stir in a full pound of honey and boil very gently for four minutes. Then strain the mess and bottle the liquid while it is still hot, taking care first of all to rinse the bottles with strong alcohol. Drink half a wineglassful of this draught after your midday meal and after supper, and it will safeguard your heart. It is said to prolong life and to keep it healthy and happy.

This wine has proved to be beneficial for those suffering from angina, high blood pressure, and general cardiac weakness.

Maid Marian's Beautifying Bath

Gather two handfuls of oak leaves and one of the leaves of the elder at Anael's hour (9–10 A.M.) on a fine spring morning. Put them into your bath with a drop of lavender oil, and you will rise from it refreshed, serene, and beautiful.

ISEWOMAN'S WEATHERBOOK

When bats flit overhead early of a summer evening and make sport with one another in the air, it is a sure sign of fair weather.

If you would read the weather, pay close attention to the leaves on the trees. If of a sudden they shake and rustle, and the breeze turns them bottoms-up, then they are foretelling a fall of rain. In the spring, if oak leaves come before the ash is green, we shall have a summer full of sunshine and cause to rejoice; but if the ash puts forth her greenery before Old Man Oak, then look out, for the summer will be of a sort that only ducks and drakes love.

❧

Peacocks are proud and royal birds and are prophets of the rain; when their haunting spirit-calls are heard over and over again, it is a warning of a wet weather soon to come.

❧

If a ladybird should alight on you, count its spots, then carefully take it on your finger and waft it up into the air, and as it flies away repeat as many times as there are spots on its back:

> Ladybird, ladybird, fly, fly away
> And give us all tomorrow a happy sunny day.

Then wait for the morrow to see if your charm will come true.

❧

When the sun is shining and there are no rain clouds, yet of a sudden a spatter of raindrops fall from the clear skies, as though it were a miracle, that is a fairy shower; and folks say that it betokens a fox's wedding.

❧

Two moons in a month bring bad weather, and there are those who say "Two moons in May means rain for a year and a day"; but folk who say so do not fully understand the significance of such a phenomenon, because two moons in May is a magical sign, and it means that the tides of life and the mysteries behind them will be high and swelling and rich for a twelvemonth or more.

Chapter Four

JUNE

The Court of Midsummer

On a Midsummer Eve

I idly cut a parsley stalk,
And blew therein towards the moon;
I had not thought what ghosts would walk
With shivering footsteps to my tune.

I went, and knelt, and scooped my hand
As if to drink, into the brook,
And a faint figure seemed to stand
Above me, with thy bygone look.

I lipped rough rhymes of chance, not choice,
I thought not what my words might be;
There came into my ear a voice
That turned a tenderer verse for me.

Thomas Hardy

ANGELS, SPIRITS, AND STARS

Cancer, the heavenly Crab,* is a creature of the lunar tides that are

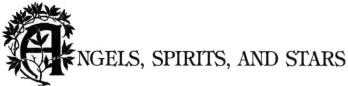

* The crab is akin to the spider, Aranea or Arachne, secret and mysterious thirteenth sign of the zodiac who climbs her shining thread to sit at the center of the cosmos— her web. The moon and the spider are both symbols for the soul.

the breath, in and out, of the great sea of all life, the boundless causal ocean that has ever been the symbol of the Great Mother. The sign is associated with those parts of the body that link the heart, the breasts, and the stomach, for the Great Mother brings forth the Child, the mystic light dwelling in the cave of the heart, and nourishes and sustains her Sun-Child (the heart is the esoteric center denoting the sun). St. Agatha, earthly representative of the mother goddess, is depicted carrying her breasts in a bowl. Receding further in time, the mists of Celtic mythology reveal that the sun is ever in danger of being swallowed by Fenris, a demonic wolf of cosmic dimensions who equates with the darkness of Brahma.

This Sun-Mother (the sun was mother as well as father to the Celts and was sometimes referred to as "she") had a beautiful daughter hidden in her disc who would one day reign supreme and create heaven and earth anew. This poetic myth seems to offer a teaching upon Cancer in its positive and negative aspects.

The beneficent influences of Cancer and its "planet," the moon, are queenly indeed. Cancer builds a protective shell in which to nurture the growth of a school, a business, a home, a caring establishment, a hospital, or a political career dedicated to the well-being of the greater home, which is the native country.

Cancer people are aware of the sheltering and protective qualities of the Great Mother and her restraining powers. The moon is royal as Isis, Astarte (traditionally, the new horned moon), Artemis, Freya, Diana, Hecate, Bride, Ceridwen, Selene, or Luna—the names are endless. Luna falls in love with the sleeping Endymion (symbol of humanity and its deeper emblem, the rising and setting sun), and it is said that when the female and male spiritual principles are truly wedded and stand side by side, the earth will be reborn. A depiction of this, and one that signifies Cancer and the Moon, is the Tree of Life, rooted in the nourishment of earthliness yet growing upward toward the sun, its branches spreading wide to shelter and embrace many birds and animals and creatures of the spirit, and fruits appearing within the cycle of its seasons. Cancer people will usually be intimately in touch with nature and bear within them the knowledge (albeit submerged) that humanity must express the harmony and wholeness inherent in the spirit of nature before the planet earth can become the true and beautiful home for all her creatures, human, plant, and animal, that the Great Plan brought into being by the goddess and the god foresaw.

Cancer is the sign of fecundity, fertility, reproduction, the goddess powers in full manifestation. The jungle, the forest, the dense wooded valley signify Cancer powers, a growth that, when headstrong and unchecked, can become unbalanced. The disease of cancer demonstrates the principle of inharmonious vigor. The moon sends her lunar tides through the human womb, and the lunar powers celebrate the great cycle of death and rebirth in humanity, in nature, in each day and each year that passes (for the twenty-four-hour cycle is a miniature drama of the grand annual pageant). The crab as a prehistoric creature of the sea seems to suggest that, indeed, the earth is still building herself and her communities from the deep primordial energies. We are still in the process of being born. The Fenris legend begins to stir here, for although we need and must celebrate physicality as a receptacle for spirit, its burgeoning qualities can appear to be enough in themselves, and so humanity begins to lose sight of its true source, home and being, which is the light of its spiritual essence.

The head of the crab is hidden, as if it represents spiritual awareness and inner wisdom. On the one hand it is a beautiful symbol, especially for Cancerians, that the source of spirit can be found deep within, in the protected and sheltered mind or soul that dwells within the heart; but in its dark aspect it signifies that the head has been lost sight of, and only the huge pincers remain, symbolizing the duality of right and left, body and soul, socialism and capitalism, male and female, intellect and emotions, through which we wend our uncomfortable way, sliding panic-stricken to one side and then veering just as dangerously and uncontrollably to the other. This lack of balance is the unfortunate result of losing sight of the spirit that provides the middle way so beloved of the Buddha and holds the powers of "good" and "evil" in perfect poise and harmony, so that their balance may create perfection and radiance and always have a positive issue.

Cancer the Crab is a sign that humanity can learn how to transcend the dualities inherent in creation only by being encased in matter—yet this very process is the symbolic Fall and gives birth to the howl of the benighted Fenris as he threatens to devour the sun in darkness (extinguish the light of the spirit or, more correctly, our awareness and response to that light). The leonine sphinx (Leo the Lion is the symbol of the sun and the heart) signals that humanity must grow the mystic head that is hidden in Cancer, the head that is evolved consciousness crowning perfected humanity, sign and symbol of godliness, human made divine. This head must grow out of the hall of learning that is the animal body or the physical experience. That body is associated with the moon, queen of matter, and the subsoil that is our emotional and subliminal self, rooted in the past of childhood and breathed over by the magic of the silvered looking glass of memory, which is the thread of continuum as we experience life inside and outside of time and space.

odiac

CANCER—CRAB
JUNE 21–JULY 22

ANGEL: Gabriel

RULING PLANET: Moon

KEYWORD: Security—sheltering, innerness, creating a sanctuary, a structure that protects and fosters

AGE: Babyhood to seven years

METAL: Silver

CROSS: Cardinal

ELEMENT: Water

QUALITIES: Reflection, sensitivity, memory, receptiveness, fluctuation, responsiveness, sympathy, magnetism

ILLNESSES TO GUARD AGAINST: Chest injuries, bronchitis, pleurisy, pneumonia, diseases of the stomach, particularly those associated with worry

BODY AREAS: Breasts, stomach, chest

STONES: Emerald, moonstone, cat's-eye, pearl, crystal

NUMBERS: 2, 7

DAY: Monday

FLOWERS AND HERBS: Poppy, water lily, white rose, watercress, moon-wort, privet

TREES: Willow, sycamore

ANIMALS: Crab, otter, seal, stag, heifer, unicorn

BIRDS: Seagull, owl, white peacock

COLORS: Pale blue, silver, pearl, glistening white, emerald green.

Cancer appears at the time of the northern midsummer sun, when, after its height, it begins to turn back again to the south but, as it were, sideways, in the fashion of a crab.

Juno, wife of Jupiter and queen of heaven, whose name bears association with the midsummer month, sent Cancer the Crab as a trial against Hercules when he was in combat with the Hydra. Cancer bit his foot (the part of the body that navigates the ship of life on its seabound voyage). Hercules killed it (released it from the prison of its body) and Juno took it up into the heavens and set it there in honor, to instruct the soul of humankind by its sign and symbol.

editation on the Moon

Choose a night of the full moon and light a silver or a white candle at Gabriel's hour (nine o'clock in the evening). Sit where you can observe the moon and begin to breathe quietly and deeply, inhaling the mystic light of her silvery rays in your imagination so that, as you breathe out, you exhale a beautiful outpouring of white magical radiance. See yourself and your surroundings as suffused with this light. Say to the moon:

> Moon-Goddess, Enchantress and Mistress of the night, I pray that I might be endued with the grace and the strength of your majesty and the beauty and enchantment of your magnetism. I experience the bliss of your peace, tranquility, and power. I hail you as Queen of Wisdom and the Receptive Soul. All my life I shall walk in the charmed circle of your wisdom, beauty, power, serenity, and mystery. I am filled with the heavenly peace of your motherly love, which enfolds me tenderly within the great white wings of Isis,* whose radiant presence is with me in every life situation.

Sit for a few moments contemplating the moon's mysteries, then bow to her and blow out your candle.

Stars of Summer

Arcturus, or the Bear-Keeper, is the great summer star shining in the group Boötes (the Herdsman). The group has seven stars, although only Arcturus is of the first magnitude. Three stars form a triangle at the top of the constellation; below this, a fourth star is in line with the majestic Arcturus (considerably larger than our sun), which itself forms a lower triangle with two smaller stars. Legend relates that Boötes invented the plow, attaching it to two oxen, so that he became known as the "ox-driver" (Homer referred to the constellation as "the wagoner"). Because of his ingenuity, he was taken up into the heavens by the gods, and he and his plough became a revered star group. The plow is a holy object in many mythologies, depicting in its deeper aspect humanity yoked to the earth and to physical toil, so that the spiritual harvest may eventually flourish. The farmer as custodian and keeper of the yielding goodness of the earth, and the earth herself as guardian of the animal body of humans, are exalted in the ideogram of the Boötes constellation with its two "keepers."

The Corona Borealis,[†] or the Northern Crown, shines to the left of Boötes, looking exactly like a mystic coronet suspended in the heavens. It was here that, in 1866, there appeared the strange phenomenon of a temporary star known as the "blaze star." One night, an Irish astronomer noted that the Northern Crown had been visited and transfigured by a mysterious brilliant stranger. Within hours, a huge cosmic conflagration had burst into being and caused the transformation of a star. What event it foretold is still a matter of dissension.

---

* You might also care to perform this meditation on one of the three "Egyptian Days" (last Monday in April, second Monday in August, third Monday of December).

† This star group is sacred to the Celtic goddess Ahrianrod.

Midsummer Eve Spell for Seeing the Fairies

Seek out a sequestered spot, wild and lovely, where all the herbs and trees of the summer flourish around you. Build a little fire in a ring of stones and smolder nine pine cones and a little incense, for these do honor to the goddess of fortune. You will have brought with you a crown twisted from oak leaves, rosemary, and wild roses, pink and white. Take only what you need from each tree or bush and bless each one for its providence.

You must wait till the twilight comes on and the stars begin to twinkle, and then dance around the fire. The fairies will show you how; listen in your heart to their inspiration, and you will dance the magical dance of the woods and the stars and the fire-bewitched night, for what was done in days of old will be done again.

When you have grown weary, sit down in a comfortable spot and dwell with deep thoughts upon the fire, which you must feed so that it springs up into life once more. Look into its flames, and ask the King of the Elves and the Queen of the Woods to be with you in your meditations. Think of the goddess and the god, and you will feel the mystical forces in nature, which are the angels and the fairies. If you keep a faithful stillness of heart, soul, and frame, you will see them dancing among the trees, and the fire will bring you visions of the spirit. As the fire burns down, lay your crown aside and intone clearly, "This is for the fairies." Then wash yourself, in your imagination, in a great shaft of light which you must see as rays coming down from highest heaven. Put out your fire and walk home to bed. Keep a pen and paper by your bedside, for your dreams will be touched with the magic of the night and the fairies.

Fairy Days and Hours

These are the times and days that you are most likely to see the fairies; be respectful, honor the little people; and mind not to stare at them, but seek to glimpse them out of the corner of your eye; be patient, for they are shyer than the wildest creatures of the woods:

Twelve o'clock noon	Bright starlit nights	Midsummer Day
Twelve o'clock midnight	New moon	Midsummer Eve
Sunrise	Hallowe'en	Christmas Day
Full moon	May Day	Christmas Eve
Early evening	Lady Day	Walpurgis Night
Dusk		

Lady Day is March 25, Midsummer Day is June 24, and Walpurgis Night is May Day Eve.

Midsummer Rose Spell

Upon Midsummer Eve, walk backwards in silence into the beauty of the evening garden and gather there a rose, the loveliest you can see. Keep it in a clean sheet of paper, without looking at it, until Christmas Day. It will be as fresh as in June; and if you place it in your bosom, he who will one day ask of you your hand and heart in marriage will at that time appear as an apparition, step forward, and take it out.

WITCH'S GARDEN

A number of herbs there are that those who would draw from the wellsprings of woman's wisdom would do well to grow in their gardens. I will tell you of some of them and how to make them flourish:

The Grass Plot

If you have a bit of grass, let daisies and clover, pink and white both, grow freely amongst its soft green blades. Do not think of uprooting every clump, for this angers the fairies. The clover leaf grows to honor the Trinity, and, if you put a leaf into your shoe, old wives say that you will be given the power to see the nature fairies and to chase the ill-natured ones away (there are some fairy beasts that dwell in darkness). If you find a four-leaf clover, keep it by you, for it will give you second sight. Red clover is good for whooping cough and bronchitis and will soothe inflammations. It will protect you from cancer and help to banish tumors. The flowers also help the headache, neuralgia, morbidity in the stomach, ulcers, and glandular problems. Eat the fresh flower heads every day that they bloom, twelve or more daily, or dry them and make a tisane.

Put four grains of wheat inside a clover leaf and wrap them up tight. Slip this charm into your bosom, and you will be able to talk to the elves.

Clover has a message for us in its leaves. Three leaves speak of eternity; four, of sweet harmony and the angels of the north, south, east, and west, who are also the angels of the elements; it is for magic and the fairies, and it is because you are in balance with Mother Nature that it helps you to see them and speak to them. Use it in your charms when you seek perfect balance. Five leaves signify fame and fortune and the beneficent ripening of your talents and plans; six bring wealth and treasures; and seven promise you a life filled with prosperity and happiness. The message of the clover is the Joy of Creation; therefore, use its flowers in your charmed potpourris to bring happiness to loved ones. In the Language of Lovers, pink clover says, "Do not trifle with my heart"; white clover promises, "I will be your true and faithful love"; and red clover begs to know, "Will you be faithful though oceans flow between us?"'

The merry little daisy should be worn on the person at midsummer, so that blessings may fall upon you in golden showers for the twelvemonth through. It will bring happiness and delight if you festoon your home with these little flowers on Midsummer's Eve. It is lucky to step upon the first daisy of the year. Daisies are so much flowers of the fairies that it was thought, in the olden days, if a baby touched that first flower, the little people would be able to steal the child away, and that if you uprooted daisies, your children would not grow. These ideas have their root in the fairies' sorrow at human destruction of the plant, so treat it well.

If a maid wishes to know how many years must pass away before she is joined in wedlock, let her find a clump of daisies with her eyes tight shut. She must count the buds and flowers, and then she will know, for each one signifies a year. If she washes her face with daisy water, which is a daisy tisane plus a little dash of honey, she will have skin as fair as milk. Make the tisane from a palmful of leaves, and it will help the circulation, safeguard the heart, and make a fine tonic. It is a good expectorant, and if you make an ointment prepared with the crushed leaves, you will have a merciful paste by you which will take the tenderness away from bruises and soothe angry inflammations. The pink daisy signifies self-effacement and simplicity, while the white daisy speaks of innocence. In the Language of Lovers it says, "I will think of it," expressing temporization.

Daisies and clover thrive on neglect.

Violet

Find a shady corner to grow a little company of violets. You will need to dig some leaf mold into the soil before planting them; and, if you can, arrange matters so that they are given as a gift; if they are given by a lover, that is even better. Keep their soil moist, and divide and replant them each spring. Harvest their flowers in the spring for charmed potpourris to cure sorrow, to foster romantic love, and to soothe nervous unease and its ailments. Gather the leaves to cure headaches, pleurisy, heart pain, diseases of the chest and lungs, swollen glands, boils, tumors and goiters. It will make a spring tonic for you if you prepare a tisane from the leaves (one tablespoonful of its chopped leaves in a half pint of spring water) and eat a few of the pretty sweet-smelling flowers every day. Do this to strengthen and calm the nerves, and for all the troubles I have listed. You will find, too, that your memory becomes sharp and clear and your mind loses its cobwebs. This tisane is an elixir; it will even help those who suffer from disorders of the blood.

If you wear its amethystine flowers around your neck, you will ward off drunkenness and all confusion of mind, for they have the same curative effects on the nervous system as does the jewel itself. If an amethyst could bloom and pour forth perfume, it would become a violet. If these shy maidens flower in the autumn, they seek to warn you to take care of your health and your person. They are said to absorb ill-willed spells and to silence the voice of evil. If you inhale their scent and contemplate their beauty, all strife and stress and vexatious thoughts will be soothed away from your mind. Blue violets mean faithfulness, the dame's violet means solicitude, the white, modesty, and the yellow, rural bliss. In the Language of Lovers, it says, "Pure and sweet art thou" and "You are my first love" (white and blue).

St. John's Wort

This is a tall plant, starred with golden-yellow flowers bright as sunshine, which stain your fingertips red as if with blood when its petals are crushed. Some folk like to say that it is the blood of John the Baptist, but the truth is that the plant is sacred to the sun and was used in the old rites on Midsummer Day. Its saffron color is also a fitting hue for St. John the Divine of the Gospels, for he is the prophet of the coming age, which will be a Golden Age.

The flowers like to grow in lime-rich soil, and they will do well with a hedge of lovage or lavender behind them. They need a spot that is partly in shade and partly bright and sunny. They will flower from late June onward, so you may harvest the flowers, leaves, and stems from then on.

St. John's wort is gentle and healing, like the Christ. Use the tisane to cure hemorrhages, to lift away pain, and to help those suffering from neuritis. It will banish madness and possession by devils and comfort hysteria. If the patient is melancholic, give her the tea, and it will be as if a heavy painful mist moves away from her and dissolves. It cleanses the lungs and the chest, and bunches of the herb hung by the bedroom door or over the sleeping couch will drive away the evil spirits that inhabit nightmares. They will bring blessings and happiness to the house, especially if a ceremony is made of hanging them at Midsummer. These flowers are beloved of Pan, and it is an old wives' tale that they used to creep about from place to place so that they would not be gathered; they are under the special protection of the Earth Angel, and it is why herb healers value them. The flowers have ever been a charm for good witchcraft and its magics. The flower is a symbol of the sun's glory and in the Language of Lovers it says, "The shining of your spirit has captured my heart."

Rosemary

This fragrant bush can be grown as a hedge or a single shrub. In the Latin, its name means "dew of the sea." It is a goddess herb, pungent, with an aroma like incense. Where the rosemary grows of its own freewill, there it is that the woman rules the house. Rosemary likes to grow in a sandy soil, light and dry; but set it where it will have protection in a hard winter. Take cuttings and foster them in sand and peat of equal parts in a sunny place. Whenever you moisten their soil, say this rune over them three times, and they will be sure to take root:

> From Christ's Sacred Heart
> Fell three drops of blood
> And Mary's tears
> Fell into the mud.
> Water, Spirit, and Body of Earth
> Bless these herbs and give them birth.

Take the cuttings in the summer, but you may harvest the fragrant branches with their needle-leaves all the year through. They are lucky for brides and soothing and calming for funeral parties.

Rosemary is a tonic for the liver and the heart and reduces the blood pressure. It will cleanse the gall bladder and take the

sickness from jaundice. For weary persons, subject to nerves, it works wonders. Invalids may be given it to help their recovery. Morbid headaches, nervous stomachs, and low spirits are banished by rosemary. It helps rheumatism, neuralgia, and sciatica when its oil is rubbed on the affected parts. Do the same for menstrual pains, but note that the tea helps as well. The infusion is very good for dullness and confusion of mind and if you are troubled with a feeling of constant drowsiness. Wash your fine and body with the tisane, and you will keep your youth. Use it as a tonic for the scalp, for it beautifies the hair. Sprigs beneath your pillow drive away troublesome dreams and anxious crowding thoughts. Add a good dose of honey to the tisane, and it will stop a cough. It is a beneficent and kindly herb, indeed. Put two teaspoonsful of the leaves in a wineglassful of boiling water and sip as soon as it is cool enough, after straining. Rosemary signifies the beautiful quality of remembrance, which is of the goddess and the moon, and in the Language of Lovers it proclaims, "Never will your precious memory fade in my heart," and, "Your vivifying presence revives me."

Chapter Five

JULY

The Month of the Rose

The Litany of the Sun

*Homage to thee, O Ra, at thy beauteous rising! Thou
risest, thou shinest at the dawn. Thou art king of the
gods. The company of the gods praise thee at sunrise
and at sunset. Thou sailest over the heights of heaven
and thy heart is glad. Thy morning boat meeteth thy
evening boat with fair wings.*

*O Thou Only One! O Thou Perfect One! O Thou who
art eternal, who art never weak, whom no mighty one
can abase. None hath dominion over things that ap-
pertain to thee.*

*Thou art unknowable, and no tongue can describe thee;
thou art alone. Millions of years have passed over the
world; I cannot tell the number through which thou
hast passed. Thou journeyest through vast spaces in a
little moment of time; thou settest and makest an end
of the hours.*

The Egyptian Book of the Dead

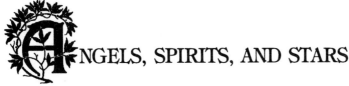

ANGELS, SPIRITS, AND STARS

The lion is the zodiacal animal that represents Leo, the sign of the sun; powerful, majestic, its tawny-gold head encompassed by the burnished flames of its mane, no better symbol could portray our day star. Yet the lion is of the cat family, creatures that were sacred to the moon cult of the Egyptians; and witches, the moon, and female magic have been associated down the ages with the cat.

The fire element, which presides over Leo as the sun (its other two chiefs being Mars and Jupiter), rules the exalted mental planes of the creative imagination, forming with the element of air the great positive life-current of the cosmos. As they bring creative impulses, so can the angels of Fire wreak terrible destruction. We can imagine Djinn, Spirit of the fire, as he is depicted in Norse myth, a fire-giant whose body is a column of writhing flames, his eyes like slanted cracks to a bottomless abyss of vermilion incandescence, sparking and flaring with the omnipotent power of his element. He is king of the salamanders, the fairy spirits of the flame who have their being in the subtle ethers but who are always present in the body of the flame itself. It is these beings who, under angelic direction, bring (together with the sylphs of the air) inspiration to artists and thinkers, anyone who is reaching up into the higher atmospheres of the mind to accomplish a task of creativity, whether that be a philosophy or a building. Yet they can also invade inharmoniously when a person gives him or herself up to irritation, stoking up this negative fire until it crackles with unholy rage and spite!

At the head of the fire hierarchy stands the Archangel Michael; he is depicted in Christian art as overcoming a dragon, perhaps the one that will eventually be set to rest in reverence at the feet of the Virgin and Child. This is Michael's task—to subdue the dragon of the elemental self, so that it may be absorbed into the power of the higher self and its holistic wisdom set free. The fire signs give a mental attitude of positive buoyancy which helps their natives (and those influenced by them) to aim for the stars of life, to rise above the petty restrictions of the lower self, to realize intuitively that the task of the Archangel is theirs also; ardor, warmth, enthusiasm, a desire to fling the past into the fire and to press on untrammeled into the glorious future is the way of the lion. So Leo people can often become great leaders, whether of a new school of thought, through their works of art, or through heading military campaigns or adventurous and risky expeditions. Their test is not to allow their natural exuberance and passion to degenerate into egotistical striving. Lucifer, the great bright spirit who became a fallen angel, is said to have brought darkness to his being by feeding its divine and celestial light into the narrow and limited channels of his ego, so gradually enclosing its wonder in the night of rigidity, isolation, and death. The lion's roar can be a hymn of praise or a snarl of savagery.

Sir George Trevelyan points out in his book *A Vision of the Aquarian Age* that in Britain's coat of arms, the crowned lion rampant stands with the unicorn, whose crown has fallen about its neck; the time may well come when Britain will re-crown her unicorn, a symbol of purified intelligence aspiring to, and receiving inspiration from, the spiritual realms. If we think of the lion and the unicorn as the sun and the moon, light is shed on the association of the lion symbol with its feline sister, the cat, creature of the moon, and on the unicorn as symbol of Christ, the Light of the World (the sun); for the moon is sister of Apollo, the sun. When she is at full tide, she represents the glorious fullness of pure wisdom and sanctified intelligence; simplistically, the lion can be seen as the positive masculine life force and the moon as the negative feminine life force (although these polarities are reversed on the inner planes, and the holistic and final truth seems to be that they are constantly flowing in and out of one another and cannot be thought of as separate).

The lesson seems again to be confirmed, for the whole world as well as Britain, that harmony can come only when the royalty of both the lion and the unicorn, side by side, is duly and equally honored. The head of Cancer the Crab (sign of the moon) must no longer be veiled, hidden, dishonored, denigrated; it must appear in glory, as it does on the leonine sphinx, growing in splendor out of the body of the lion; thus the lower and the higher selves are brought into harmony, perfect vehicles for one another. The creative forces enter the soul of humanity unbeguiled by imbalance and duality, and Archangel Michael's task is done.

As the sun's archetype, Apollo appears in myth as a golden youth whose radiant gaze destroyed all that was not true and honest. His glance dispelled illusion and glamour. He carried a lyre and bow, and sent shafts of his divine sunshine into the deepest shadows of earth and humanity. Like the lion, his aspect was beautiful and terrible. The lies of life must be swept away; the dragon of the conceit-loving ego must die. The lion has claws, but the sun is the symbol of rebirth, for it rises anew every morning, and its death in midwinter is followed by its splendid return. Apollo was a god of divination and prophecy, for, as the eyes of the sphinx gaze calm and unwavering on the equinoctial sunrise, so can those most influenced and empowered by the sun behold glorious visions of the future, gazing into the light without being dismayed by the shifting mists, shadows, and gloom that might transiently prevail in the middle distance. Pride was the fault of Apollo, for, although he signified humanity's heart of hearts—the spiritual sun that shines behind the mundane manifestation in the heavens and in the human body—that shining center could sometimes illuminate a powerful individualism that perverts free will into self-will and the desire to dominate. The wolf, the griffin, and the crow are sacred to Apollo.

The leonine lion as symbol of the imperishable spirit in humanity is associated with the tradition that the whelp of the lion is born dead, remaining so for three days until the father breathes on it. This story reflects that of the Resurrection, when Christ rose on the third day, and also gives intimations of the passage of the soul into heavenly realms upon the death of the body. According to the Tibetans, the period in which the soul detaches itself from its earthly prison, after the body has died, is three days.

The lion heads that spout water in fountains and pools were originally conceived in Egypt, because it was during the month governed by Leo that the Nile was inundated. Today, Leo's zodiacal reign still heralds the "Dog Days" that begin on July 3 (ending on August 11). These are the hottest part of the summer, when, according to the ancient Romans, the Dog Star, or Sirius (meaning "sparkling star") rises with the sun and adds to its heat.

odiac

LEO—LION
JULY 23–AUGUST22

ANGEL: Mikael or Michael
RULING PLANET: Sun

KEYWORD: Creativity

AGE: Every stage of life

METAL: Gold

CROSS: Fixed

ELEMENT: Fire

QUALITIES: Initiation, power, glory, vigor, ardor, beneficence, creative force, self-expression, full of ideas, talent

ILLNESSES TO GUARD AGAINST: Injuries to the heart, eyes, back, and spine; weakness of the heart, angina, spinal afflictions, lumbago, eye diseases

BODY AREAS: Heart

STONES: Amber, chrysolite, tourmaline, topaz, sardonyx, ruby, diamond

NUMBERS: 1, 4

DAY: Sunday

FLOWERS AND HERBS: Marigold, sunflower, cowslip, heliotrope, hops, peony

TREES: Palm, laurel, pine, oak

ANIMALS: Lion, wolf, griffin

BIRDS: Peacock, cock, eagle

COLORS: All shades of gold, yellow, orange, vermilion, copper, blood red, light green, white

Leo is called after the symbol of the sun; it is the lion, king of all beasts, including the animal body of humans. So Leo is king of physicality.

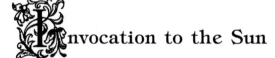 nvocation to the Sun

Light a candle at Michael's hour (4 A.M., 12 noon or 8 P.M.) or at midnight, 3, 6, or 9 o'clock. Rest your eyes on the golden flame and think of the radiant solar disc, remembering that everything on earth is a manifestation of the magical rays of the sun. Then say:

> Archangel Michael, I am aware of your golden presence as you lead me into the light, into the heart of the sun behind which shines the inscrutable spiritual sun,

the beating Heart of Love around which all the planets, moons, and suns of the universe revolve. I contemplate this mystery and blend with the brilliant white radiance of the spiritual sun, which fills all my being with every in-breath and flows out to bless the world with every out-breath.

Stars of Summer

Appearing above and to the left of the Northern Crown is the constellation Hercules, sporting four stars that form a noticeable quadrilateral. The star group is a complex configuration, consisting of twenty-eight stars stretching out from the central square. Close by, almost as if it were the heart of Hercules, is the globular star-cluster known as Messier 13 (visible only through binoculars or a telescope). It is a marvelous piece of celestial jewelry, harboring many thousands of stars.

The most important star in Hercules is Ras Algethi, a cool red super giant that is actually a double star. Ras Algethi is possibly the largest known star.

It is believed that Hercules once walked the earth and was a type of pre-Christ figure, akin to the Indian Arjuna, the earthly pilgrim or disciple.* Hercules was said to be the avatar of a long-distant Taurean Age, and his Twelve Labors represent the twelve labors each soul has to make on earth before passing on to a new and more evolved cycle. Each labor consists of many lives in the successive ages of the great wheel of the zodiac as it turns above the earth; the twelve labors are the consummation for every individual soul of the Great Cosmic Year.

The Twelve Labors of Hercules were as follows: to slay the Nemean lion; to slaughter the Lernean hydra; to capture alive the Arcadian stag; to kill the Erymanthian boar; to clean the stables of King Augeas; to annihilate the cannibal birds of the Lake Stymphalus; to take as captive

---

*Hercules's connection to the earth is emphasized by the fact that in the region of his constellation, the stars are generally approaching the earth, while the ones that lie opposite to him are receding from it.

the Cretan bull; to capture the horses of the Thracian Diomedes; to bring back the girdle of Hippolyta; to bring back the cattle of Geryon; to purloin the precious apples of the Hesperides, and to rescue from the infernal regions the three-headed dog Cerberus. The name Hercules means "the Kneeler," an indication of the spiritual devotion by which he undertook the Twelve Labors so that he might achieve immortality.

Cultivation of Herbs

IN THE GARDEN

Choose a southwest position for your herb garden and surround it with a hedge to screen it from winter storms and summer gales. Lovage can be grown as a hedge, as can lavender, sage, rosemary, and the apothecaries' rose (Rosa gallica officinalis). While the hedge is growing, climbing plants trained up a trellis (nasturtiums and sweet peas, for instance) will give some protection.

Where most herbs are concerned, nature and her elements will do much of the work for you; however, if the site you have selected for cultivating herbs has poor soil, dig in peat. If the soil is heavy and moisture-retaining, put the peat in at the end of autumn. Such a soil will also need the addition of coarse sand to improve drainage. If your soil is fine and dry, just add peat six weeks before planting or sowing. Take note of the tides of the moon.

Waxing Moon (growing to full): sow seeds that are quick to germinate three days after the new moon; those that germinate slowly should be sown the day after Bride's or Astarte's crescent has risen anew in the night skies.

Waning Moon (diminishing to darkness): plant during the evening in a waning moon, for the fluid in living things falls during this phase of the moon; the water will go down to the roots to nourish them and make them strong.

Try out one or two of the wisewoman's charms for growth and her prayers for calling forth special blessings from the angels and the fairies. These will help plants that are reluctant to establish themselves.

During a bitter and prolonged winter, it is necessary to protect some herbs from the cold; these are hyssop, lavender, rosemary, bay, and sage. Spread a thick mulch to help the roots and enclose the bushes in evergreen cuttings bound round with polyethylene sheeting tied well against the wind. Remove the wraps as soon as the frost relents.

When spring comes, check sowing times for your seeds and resist the temptation to sow too early before weather conditions are really favorable. Prepare the soil by breaking up the lumps at the time of the waning moon (in its last week) and then, after the new moon, repeat the process and rake with vigor, spending enough time to refine the soil to a pastry-crumb structure. Sow your seeds sparingly in a shallow furrow, no more than half an inch deep even for the largest type of seed, and cover them over thinly. If you are in doubt about the quality of the soil (even after all your efforts), then put in some seed compost (soilless).

If you have established perennial herbs, check to see how they have come through the winter. If they look unhappy, try one of the healing methods described in the wisewoman's journal. It will be as well to take further cuttings from mature plants, however; these are normally best propagated in the summer, but don't be afraid to gather a few cuttings in the spring if you think it necessary. Take semiripe shoots, about 8 cm or 3 inches long, use rooting powder, and put them in little pots containing equal parts of sand and peat, leaving them in a warm shady place protected from frosts, sun, and wind. Take care not to let them dry out.

Once all the young plants under your care have established themselves and are growing well, you need only thin the seedlings and hoe around them gently, watering if the weather is very dry or hot. Talking to plants, encouraging them to flourish and praising their efforts, is highly recommended. As you develop a special friendship with the herbs in your garden, they will send forth their aromas to greet you as you walk by.

GROWING HERBS IN CONTAINERS

Herbs grown indoors need plentiful light, a good compost, and an adequate supply of moisture. Water well once a week, or more often if the weather is very hot. Regular watering every day tends to rot herbs, so allow them time to dry out between waterings, even during a heat wave. Avoid blinding sunlight on window ledges; move the herbs away from a south-facing window during brilliant summer weather. Use clay pots to allow excess water to evaporate, as plastic ones do not permit this process. It is better to allow them to stand on a layer of gravel in a tray, as this will provide them with better drainage and humidity.

Herbs flourish in larger containers such as troughs, window boxes, and barrels. Place them away from windy spots and line the bottom of their containers with broken crocks (fragments of clay pot) with the curved sides uppermost. Add some charcoal to these to benefit the soil. Form a cylinder with wire netting and stand it in the center, building up the compost around it. Plant the herbs around the mouth of this cylinder and water the plants down the center once a week or more often, as necessary. This will ensure that the water is fed into the soil evenly. Dig in some well-rotted compost each spring but avoid further feeding, as this can adversely affect the herbs' aroma and concentration of essential oils, minerals, and nutrients. Don't be afraid to cut what you need from the herbs, as this will make their growth hardier and more dense, but harvest their leaves and flowers within a few days of the new moon if you wish to take them in quantity. Cutting during the waxing moon will promote growth, while pruning done as the moon wanes inhibits it.

ISEWOMAN'S JOURNAL

The Language of the Rose

Red rose—Love purified by suffering; lovers use it to say I love you,

White rose—The rose of perfect peace; for lovers it declares refusal—"I love you not,"

Yellow rose—The rose of joy and a sunlit heart; in the Language of Lovers it represents misplaced affection—"I love another,"

Moss rose—The sweetness of humility; for lovers, shy love—"My admiring gaze rests on you from afar,"

Pink rose—Affection and human warmth; for lovers "My love

is innocent and pure and stems from a disinterested heart,"

Orange rose—Vigor and vitality; for lovers it proclaims "Let us rejoice in the springtime of our love";

Amethyst rose—Calmness and poise of spirit and heart; for lovers, it says "None could ever turn my heart from you,"

Wild rose—The spirit of woman; it speaks to lovers of maidenly beauty—"You are as fair and as innocent as this flower."

Roses have a mystic language that can only be learnt when one sits in deep contemplation of them. Do so every day, and they will speak to your heart.

Remember the angels of the hours and the days, and indeed the angelic host in its glorious infinity, for the angels will help to reveal to you the mystical essence of the rose.

Author's Note

From the depths of time the rose has been considered the queen of flowers, akin to holy books and teachings in its symbol of evolved spirituality and in its magical perfection of form and fragrance—a sort of guru of the garden. The Rosicrucians (Brothers of the Rosy Cross) believed that the rose signified the ultimate flowering of the spirit when the lower self of humanity was stretched in sacrifice on the cross of matter so that the star of light within the heart shone forth in radiance and the rose bloomed upon the cross, transmuting all pain and anguish to heavenly ecstasy; so the rose was matter made divine.

The story of St. Rosalia tells how she was carried by angels to a wild and lonely mountain, where she dwelt for many years in the cleft of a rock, a portion of which she wore away with her knees in offering her devotions. The picture is such a perfect representation of the beleaguered soul struggling to attain perfection of the spirit (while enclosed in the severities of matter) that it seems only fitting that she is depicted in art as in a cave with a cross and skull (the skull representing the death and sacrifice of the lower self on the cross), and then, her mission accomplished, she is shown in the act of receiving a rosary or chaplet or roses from the Virgin.

St. Mary Magdalen's Rose Philter for a Broken Heart

It is well to prepare this philter in July, when the soft sweet airs of summer celebrate the loving and gentle presence of the goddess. St. Mary Magdalen is her earthly counterpart, in one of her many guises, so the rose is St. Mary Magdalen's flower. Look for her in the old paintings of the saints, and you will see her young and lovely with an abundance of flowing hair, holding in her hands a box of healing ointment. She is the patron saint of penitents, and she bears within her the healing qualities of the goddess.* Hers is the task of comforting, soothing, and binding wounds of both the body and the soul. If it be that you are broken in heart or spirit, drink of this philter and be whole again.

---

* Her famous healing oil was spikenard, with which she anointed the head of the Christ as he sat to eat with Simon the Leper.

6 cups of red rose petals
6 cups of white rose petals
6 cups of petals taken from
wild rose bushes or from the
briar, either pink or white
1 cup of yellow rose petals

3 pounds of honey
2 tablespoonsful of
raspberry vinegar
1 ounce of yeast
1 gallon of spring
or well water

Gather the petals at Anael's hour (1 A.M., 9 A.M., or 5 P.M.), calling down blessings from the goddess as you work. Let the fairies know what you are about, and they will add their magic to your efforts. Take two quarts of the water, put it in a bowl, and steep the rose petals therein for two days, leaving the bowl covered with a white linen cloth. On the third day, mix half of the honey in a quart of boiling water, let it cool, and add the mellifluent liquid to the rose-petal water, doing this at Raphael's hour (7 A.M., 3 P.M., or 11 P.M.). Later on the same day, put in the raspberry vinegar and the yeast and leave the philter alone again for nine days, straining well upon the sixth day and then again on the ninth.

Boil up the rest of the honey in the last quart of water (let it bubble and dance upon the stove for only a second or two) and add it to the mixture when it is cool, observing the same hour as before. Cover the glass bowl or jar closely once again with the linen cloth, binding the whole tightly so that nothing from the air may intrude upon the purity of your philter. Leave it in a warm place until there is no more fermentation, upon which you may bottle it in rose-colored glass, if you can, and drink it as you please. It is better drunk in a waning moon, and, if you can heat a little rose oil and inhale its fragrance as you imbibe, that is all the better. You may intone this charm as you drink:

> Gentle Mother, within the Rose
> Hear my prayers and soothe my woes
> As I drink this red rose heart
> Bless me with your healing art.

WITCH'S GARDEN

The Wild Rose

Grow the lovely briar rose in your garden, for of all nature's treasures it is among the most wonderful. Every human life on earth is attended with suffering and the gentle enchantment of the wild rose is placed by the hand of the divine in the wilderness for our delight and well-being, our comfort and healing. Its country name is the dog rose, so called because it is said to cure rabies, but I would turn the letters about and call it by its true name, God's rose.

Take cuttings during the early summer from bushes both pink and white that grow in the wild, for it is a delight to behold the maidenly purity of the white flowers and the blush of the Venus-pink roses waving together in the summer breeze. Put the cuttings in peat and sand in a pot that will give them good drainage, and water them every day. If you can pour upon them rosemary water, nettle water, or rose water, that is all the better (these waters are the dregs of the tisanes, but they must not be dark or cloudy). The cuttings must be encouraged to grow in a warm spot that is yet protected from the full fierce glare of the sun. Say the growing-charm over them, but this spell must also be spoken for each one:

> I ask a fairy from the wild
> Come and tend this wee rose-child
> A babe of air she thrives today
> Root her soul in God's good clay
> Fairies, make this twig your bower
> By your magic shall Time see her flower.

Take care not to mutter the words as if they had no meaning, but speak them from your heart, with a true prayer on your lips for fairy cooperation, for it is only the nature folk who can bring life to your rose slips. Look out to see whether one of the little people makes its abode near your cutting. You will tell from the new life and vigor that the shoot begins to possess. Then you will know that it cannot help but take root.

When they are growing hardily, transplant them to a nook in your garden that has a little shade, such as a group of trees or a wall, but is otherwise sunny. The young rose bushes will need a rich soil that does not become waterlogged, so dig some sand into the earth that will receive their roots and put in a generous amount of peat, also. Compost from your own heap is especially good.

The blooms of the briar rose may be used in a tisane or eaten fresh, to brew a tonic for the heart, the brain, the kidneys, to cure catarrh and women's disorders, and to help the stomach. Take of the leaves also in the same way, and they will take the anger out of any heat or painful inflammation within the body or of the skin. Put the leaves and the rose blooms in your bath, and drink of the tea while taking it, to restore your spirits, sweeten your dreams, and revive tired hopes and lost visions. Take the tea to foster beauty within and without, and drink of and wash with the rose water everyday that you may put a bloom on your complexion as fair as the wild rose itself. Rose water may be made from garden roses as well as the briar. Fill a pan with petals, put in rainwater, spring water, or water from the well, bring to the boil, simmer gently for three minutes, and strain away the transparent petals. When preparing the tisane, use a china pot or earthenware vessel, add rose leaves as well as the blooms, and infuse for only one minute, in the usual way. To add a dash of honey is a good thing, unless it should be that your kidneys are in a very morbid state, in which case, drink the blessed rose tisane just as it comes, fresh from the pot and from nature, and offer thanks for its virtues.

Chapter Six

AUGUST

Lammas Tide: Festival of the First Fruits

In Praise of the Virgin

Of one that is so fair and bright,
Velut maris stella
Brighter than the dayės light,
Parens et puella,
I cry to thee; thou see to me!
Lady, pray thy son for me,
Tam pia,
That I motė come to thee,
Maria.

Lady, flower of allė thing,
Rosa sine spina
Thou borė Jesu, heavenės king
Gratia divina.
Of allė thou bear'st the prize,
Lady, queen of Paradise
Electa.
Maidė mildė mother is
Effecta.

Anonymous

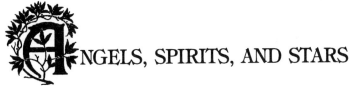

ANGELS, SPIRITS, AND STARS

Astrologically, Virgo's image is that of a young woman holding a flower, a sheaf of corn, or some other emblem of the flowering earth with which she is associated. In one sense, Virgo is the Earth Angel, working under the direction and inspiration of the Divine Mother or goddess aspect of the godhead, whose special task it is to create a nurturing environment for the young souls who need to flock to earth like migrating birds to learn through their mystic experiences in matter the secrets of spiritual mastership. The angelic hierchy streams forth as a creation of the goddess, structuring the earth and the heavens so that every soul is provided with an estate (the "right to be here"), enabling him or her to function on the earth plane. The great Earth Angel (one of the four mighty archangels of the elements) directs the angels or devas who serve her in the building of physical form as it is born, flourishes, dies, and is recycled in the material bodies of humanity, plants, animals, and the mineral kingdom. She holds a mystic loom on which she weaves the spell of creation, and it is this spiritual metaphor that has made sacred the image of the Spinning Woman, revered in many religion-inspired mythologies.

In her role as the Earth Angel it is not surprising to find that Virgo is often portrayed holding a five-petaled flower or a sheaf of wheat with five ears, for five is the number of the earthly senses and of the digits of the hand. Mercury, which rules Virgo, also rules the hands, and it is these that perform the craftwork of building on the material plane. So Virgo people love to work with their hands to create beautiful forms, delighting in the arts and crafts and in providing nourishing food, which they prepare with great care, paying attention to health, hygiene, and diet. They are drawn to herbalism and healing and make excellent nurses and doctors. They are sensitive to the etheric, fairy life of the planet and with the right attunement can easily enjoy soul-communication with nature spirits. They usually need to learn not to be so engrossed by details that they lose sight of the holistic plan that is their greater purpose, and to remember that the vital, earthy energies upon which they draw are a part of a greater strength, a greater light, which embraces all creation and in which their true being is sourced. By these means they will be able to overcome the feelings of anxiety and inadequacy which often afflict them when they forget that there is more to life and themselves than the earth, with which they are so much in harmony.

The five ears of wheat or the five-petaled flower also link Virgo with the five-pointed star or pentagram, associated with the secret elixir or quintessence of the alchemists. Whereas the ancient Greeks declared that there were four elements in which matter could exist, the Pythagoreans added a fifth—ether—purer and more subtle than fire and endowed with an orbicular motion; ether was said to have flown upward at creation and to have formed the stars as the fifth essence (therefore quintessence), the most subtle extract of a body that can be procured.

Such a magical notion inspired the alchemists whose task it was to discover the spirituality in nature and matter; so they created essences "five times distilled" as an esoteric principle. Horace links Venus with the Earth-Goddess, Earth Angel, Divine Mother, and Virgin Mary when he speaks of "kisses which Venus has imbued with the quintessence of her own nectar."

The idea of the maiden or mother weaving the spell of creation on a loom is further depicted in medieval images of Virgo in which she is to be seen wielding a distaff, symbol of the Spinning Woman or Maiden. When Gabriel visited the Virgin Mary to announce that she was to give birth to the Christ, Mary was employed in spinning flax, the Mother's task of bringing the Light (*Christ* means "Light") down to earth, into matter. That the corn with which Virgo is always associated is the Christ, the Bread of Life or the Light in Matter, is indicated by the fact that, in art, the Virgin Mary appears studded with ears of corn, whereas Virgo, the stellar goddess, is studded with stars. Medieval icons often show Mary with a star on her brow and one on her shoulder, a possible indication that spiritual inspiration and illumination of the higher faculties must be earthed in matter—the shoulders intimating the burden and sheer toil of such a mission. These stars make a link with Virgo in that the great bright powerful fixed star of the constellation is Spica ("ear of wheat"), again connecting Christ as the Light of the World and the Bread of Life (the masculine and feminine principles in Christ).

The genesis of Virgo is found in ancient Egypt, where the Corn Maiden is none other than the goddess Isis, her dress flowing with stars, holding either a wand of office (interchangeable with the distaff, as her office is to weave creation) or the child Horus, who represents the Eye of God (this eye is always portrayed singly and is a symbol of the Third Eye, that center of consciousness that is said to lead from earthly understanding to divine apperception of the cosmos).

The Greek myths surrounding the Corn Maiden are not so old. It is not surprising that, bypassing the passion and the poetry of the gods as they did for the world of concepts and ideas, the Greeks should have instigated stories of the Maiden that show her in difficult relationships with her patriarchal father; these have little to do with the deeper truths and mystical illumination with which the Egyptians and, later, the Christians were concerned.

There is a further mystery to be unveiled, in that Gabriel (the Angel of the Moon, mother of matter and dreams) came to tell Mary the good news. In astrology, the earth and water elements are closely linked, and both represent the Mother (Earth is an anagram for "heart"). It would seem fitting, then, that Gabriel visited Mary. The womb of the Earth Mother contains the seed of Light that will discover unto humanity the essence of its spiritual nature. Such is Gabriel's message. But Gabriel herself has another guise, the guise of Mercury. Mercury is the archetypal messenger of the gods, the messenger, in particular, of Jupiter. In his book *Esoteric Astrology*, Alan Leo teaches that the angels connected with the Earth element work in the sphere of the influence of Jupiter (the planet Jupiter being a vehicle, a receiving and transmitting station for one of the seven rays of creation) and that Jupiter, coming himself under the influence of the Earth Angel, is the Lord of Form on all planes (thereby revealing him as the Dagda of the Celts, who intuitively grasped this esoteric truth). Mercury, in his own right a channel for a cosmic being, is associated with the air element; but the greater entity, whom he serves, is actually connected with the earth element and with the mutable quality of wisdom, so linking with Virgo, the Great Mother.

Christ was born into the Piscean age and was its avatar. The relationship between him and his mother is expressed, in astrological terms, in that Virgo and Pisces are on opposite sides of the zodiac, so contemplating one another in adoration. In the Middle Ages Virgo's imagery was linked with the Grail symbolism by substituting the maiden for a holy chalice (the Cup of the Holy Grail). This seems to make sense in the light of King Arthur's supernatural message concerning the mystery of the Grail: "You and the land (the earth) are one." So the symbolism appears here in another guise, and another truth is indicated: the Chalice is the womb, the Great Mother, the Earth herself; humanity stands revealed as her ultimate offspring. Through the auspices of the Green revolution, the King and the earth shall be shown to be one; then, and only then, may the Golden Age begin anew.

In the great cycles of the zodiac, a year is 26,000 earth years in length. Each of the twelve signs takes 2,000 years or more to pass through its respective age. Virgo belongs to the great zodiacal winter, where she is revered in the midwinter cult of the Virgin and Child, although she is Corn Goddess of the divine harvest (quite aptly), according to her occurrence in late July, the beginning of harvest time and a herald of the magical harvest moon. But, as the midwinter Virgin, she brings forth the child of spring, which, in terms of the zodiacal ages, is Leo, golden heart of the springtime and signal of the rebirth of a Golden Age. If the Earth herself is the virgin, and humanity the vehicle for her solar child, it is interesting that the age of brotherhood (our present age of Aquarius) is gazed tranquilly upon (as the Virgin and Christ are said to do because of the position of Virgo and Pisces) by its opposite zodiacal number—the golden Leo.

In ancient Celtic custom, this linkage of the Corn Maiden in Virgo, goddess of fruits, flowers, ripened corn, and the summer harvest, with the solar child, was (and still is) celebrated in Britain by the making of the Kern Baby, woven from the last few stalks of the harvest in the cornfields. This baby harbored the spirit of the Corn Maiden or Earth Goddess whom it was vital not to insult with disrespectful behavior. Her presence needed to be recognized, respected, and loved.

odiac

VIRGO—VIRGIN
AUGUST 23–SEPTEMBER 22

ANGEL: Raphael
RULING PLANET: Mercury

KEYWORD: Operation

AGE: 7–14 years (youth)

METAL: Platinum and quicksilver

CROSS: Mutable (the Child)

ELEMENT: Earth

QUALITIES: Practicality, discernment, intelligence, healing (health, hygiene, diet), duty, fundamentals, craftsmanship, purity

ILLNESSES TO GUARD AGAINST: Ailments of the abdomen and intestines, digestive debility

BODY AREAS: Abdomen, intestines

STONES: Cornelian, jade, diamond, jasper, aquamarine, olivine, tourmaline

NUMBERS: 5, 10

DAY: Wednesday

FLOWERS AND HERBS: Rosemary, Madonna lily, cornflower, valerian

TREES: Hazel, elder

ANIMALS: Cock, squirrel

BIRDS: Magpie, parrot

COLORS: Pastel shades of blue, gold, peach yellow, and amethyst; jade green; autumn hues

Astraea, goddess of justice, lingered longest on earth of all the dieties and, on returning to heaven, became the constellation Virgo (the Maiden or Virgin).

Meditation on Mercury

Light a candle at Raphael's hour (7 A.M., 3 P.M., or 11 P.M.) and meditate on the quicksilver Messenger of the Gods:

> Lord Mercury, I perceive your lightning spirit within
> the precincts of my inner vision. I recognize that you
> are the soul of discernment, wisdom, and healing, the

communicator of thoughts and inspiration from the higher mental planes, where divine intelligence resides. I behold you in your eternal youth, a playful prankster who yet wields the caduceus of wisdom and healing, your robes of silver, your sandals winged, your eyes dancing with the infinite lights of the illumined intellect, your golden hair crowned with a wreath of olive leaves, ivy, and mulberries.

As emissary of the sun, I ask you to help me in my endeavors; let me receive the draught of your inspiration, the speed and ease of your quicksilver thoughts, your ready grasp of ideas, concepts, and all intellectual challenge. Clear the clinging mists away from my mind; let my mind be as penetrating, as muscular and indefatigable as the spirit of Mercury. Let my mind be as wise, discerning, and lucid in its discrimination as the power of the staff you uphold. Bringer of the sunlight, Lord Mercury, let the light shine in every corner of my mental body, so that I am strong, wise, and healthy in mind, tempered with humility and illumined in the acknowledgment of my status as an ignorant child of the universe.

Say the prayer three times and then contemplate its imagery and meaning in silence until Raphael's hour passes away.

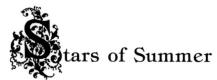# Stars of Summer

Above Hercules occur the two constellations, Serpens ("the serpent") and Ophiuchus ("the serpent bearer"). These two groups intersect one another, for they represent the mythic figures of the Serpent and the Serpent Bearer as they engage in mortal combat, the serpent coiled around his foe, who seeks to slay him. The star Alpha Ophiuchi is very close to Hercules's Alpha Herculis, while the Serpens star group may be traced from just below the Northern Crown in the space between Hercules and Boötes.

Lower in the skies from the Serpent and his Bearer are Libra, Scorpio, and Sagittarius. Libra lies below Virgo and to the east of the Corn Maiden. Look for a triangle to identify it.

Scorpio lies next to Libra and is more conspicuous. In southern latitudes, Scorpio appears as a brilliant treasury of stars immersed in a luminous and glittering stretch of the magical Milky Way, but, sadly, observers in northern latitudes are unable to see the whole constellation. Look for a curve of stars, and especially for its Alpha star (of the first magnitude), which is called Antares or Ant-Ares, because its fiery rubescene makes it the rival of Ares, or Mars (Ant-Ares meaning literally "rival of Mars"). It is one of the largest stars.

Sagittarius can be found to the left of Scorpio and higher up in the heavens. It is fainter than its neighbor, although the Milky Way in its vicinity shines with a strange haunting beauty in the dusky evenings of later summer. It is in Sagittarius that the mysterious stellar center is hidden—a dense, vast cluster around which it is thought that the entire galactic system revolves.

The constellation Lyra (the Lyre) can be found to the left of Hercules. It is recognizable by its lower quadrilateral and its upper equilateral triangle. Its most brilliant star is Vega ("falling"), which forms part of the triangle. Vega is one of the brightest stars of the heavens, fifty times more powerful than our sun.

The lyre is one of the most poetic images of mythology. The Celtic Dagda brings the seasons into being with his lyre or harp; Orpheus charmed savage beasts and the wild thrashing of the elements with his; Hercules and Apollo used lyres to perform similar miracles, and Amphion's magical lyre moved stones so that they built Thebes of their own volition. The teaching behind these ancient stories posits that the essence of creation is music.

ISEWOMAN'S JOURNAL

Cakes for the Queen of Heaven

At Lammas-tide, which falls on the calends of August, it is good to make a charmed bread and invite your friends to your home to celebrate this Festival of the First Fruits.

Make the bread in the usual way, but, as you knead and pound the dough, you must sing gaily and thump into the goodness of the grain all the goodness of your heart until you see it overflowing with happiness. Whisper this rune:

> Three angels walked by my door
> And one came after—
> Gentle Sachiel to grant me laughter.
> Four angels walk by my door
> Joy live here forevermore.

All the comfort and good cheer that is in your spirit must be put into your baking so that you may cast your bread upon the waters. When your friends and family sit with you at your board, and you eat the fruits of your labor (which shall be bread and the fruits of the earth), merrymaking will spread like a craze among you, and you will want to end the night with dancing and singing.

The Yarrow Lovespell

Take the leaves of the yarrow, which is the maiden's herb and a blessing for mothers and all women, having qualities that comfort, heal, and protect; and tickle the inside of the nostrils, murmuring to yourself this old country charm:

> Green yarrow, green yarrow, you bear a white bow;
> If you love me, love me, my nose will bleed now;
> If my love don't love me, it won't bleed a drop,
> If my love do love me, 'twill bleed every drop.

Girdle of Venus

These sweet-smelling dried herbs and flowers are charmed and sacred to the goddess and will always evoke her presence. In breathing their perfume, you will be mystically enchanted by the virtues of the goddess and so emanate her sweetness, goodness, beauty, and simplicity, her magics and her holy powers of healing, creation, and magnetism. Gather together these herbs and flowers upon an altar under the August new moon:

Blackberry leaves	Rose petals	Daisy heads	Corn violets
Raspberry leaves	Rose leaves	Meadowsweet	Yarrow
Lavender sprigs	Rose buds	Birch bark	Elder leaves

They must all be ready dried, and you must be sure to use the three rose ingredients so that they make up about one-half of your mixture. Stir all together in a crystal bowl and use nought but a wooden spoon. Add cloves, a good tablespoonful of cinnamon, one of nutmeg, and one of orris root (all of them ground to powder) and heap your spoon for each, except the cinnamon. As you stir, you must say:

> Fair moon bright above me
> Bring visions of the goddess lovely
> Blessed Lady of fruits and flowers
> Breathe upon these sacred hours
>
> These leaves from trees, these herbs and flowers
> Make holy with your living powers
> Raise the power! Bestow the magic!
> Set Earth's seal upon my magic!
> Set Anael's seal upon my magic!
> May goddess-power seal my magic!
> This I ask tonight of thee;
> A pure flowing channel may I be
> As I receive, may I give again
> Holy waters of Ceridwen.

As you supplicate the goddess, you must see her come into the place where you have your altar as though she walked berobed into a holy grove, there to greet you and instruct you in her magic. You must see yourself receiving in reverence and then giving of your own soul's essence, so that your work is for the blessing and healing of the world, for it is the goddess's world. Remember this. You must work to bless her flowers and trees, her stones and waters, the living soil, her birds and beasts, her humanity, every member of the human family. Only thus will you be filled with the power.

Now take your bowl and light a white candle and scatter a little of your charmed mixture to the fairies, as an offering and a sign of good will, and as a prayer that they might instill their own fragrant force and vigor into the magic recipe. Take the bowl of herbs, flowers, and leaves to your bedchamber and light your candle again at Raphael's hour (the hour before midnight). Stir into it six good drops of rose oil, rubbing it into the mixture with your bare hands (which should be washed and clean) and chanting again the charm as you work. Infuse the mixture with bright streaming washes of color from your soul, which should pour forth in shades of viridian green, Egyptian turquoise and softest rose-petal pink.

Have a bag of coarse-grained salt ready to hand and a jar of green, blue, pink, or clear glass (colored is better). Begin to separate the charmed mixture into layers inside the jar. Nine layers must there be, and nine times must each be sprinkled with the salt, before being covered with the next layer, as you intone the charm all the while. As you cover the last layer with salt, make the sign of the cross upon the mixture as though you drew it with a vivid silver pen from which ink of purest silver flows. Now stopper up the jar so that it is airtight, and make a circle of radiant candles around it. Say the charm again, and blow them out as you finish. Put the jar in a secret place, dim and warm, and wait for June's new moon. On that mysterious night, bring forth the fragrant flowers and herbs and put them into a casket, sitting quietly to absorb the intoxicating magic of their potent perfume. You will be infused and inspired with the spirit of the goddess, and you will go forth to do works, to bring joy and healing and ecstasy, in her name and under her star.

Flora's Dial and the Angels of the Hours

There is a dial from olden times that shows a clockface of flowers that open and close in harmony with the angels of the hours. The hours are the measured heartbeats of the mother-spirit that is our earth, and they are sacred; her flowers and herbs, grasses and trees grow in accordance with her rhythms. They have magical virtues and healing properties and are for the free use of all who need them.

MORNING	FLOWER	RULING ANGELS
One o'clock	Sow thistle closes: a tisane for the skin, eye inflammations and as a tonic for the liver.	Anael and Bne Seraphim
Two o'clock	Yellow goatsbeard opens: use the yellow dried flowerheads in potpourri for charms dedicated to happiness and well-being.	Auriel or Uriel
Three o'clock	Common oxtongue opens: use the leaves and the juice of the flowers in salads as a blood tonic.	Cassiel and Agiel
Four o'clock	Late dandelion opens: use the raw leaves and especially the juice in the hollow stem for all liver and skin disorders and as a diuretic and laxative; it will cure kidney complaints and biliousness.	Michael and Nachiel
Five o'clock	Red poppy opens: the juice from the seedhead will gently induce sleep; the leaves and petals in a tisane will soothe an infected throat or chest. Use for all respiratory complaints, particularly asthma and hay fever.	Gabriel and Malcha Betharsisim
Six o'clock	Cat's-ear* opens: use in charmed potpourri for bringing happiness to the home.	Samael and Graphiel
Seven o'clock	Marigold opens: use this plant as a tisane—flowers and leaves—to treat cancer and other tumors; it will make a comforting eyewash as well. Make an ointment from the marigold to treat cuts, bruises, burns, stings, and boils, and use the dried heads in potpourri, charmed for good health.	Raphael and Tiriel

* No known healing properties.

MORNING	FLOWER	RULING ANGELS
Eight o'clock	Pink opens: use the pink as a dried flower in all your potpourri recipes for love and tender romance, and especially use the petals of the clove-scented pink for flavoring to make Sweetheart's Junket.	Sachiel and Johphiel
Nine o'clock	Field marigold opens: use as for the dandelion—both flowers will bring a bloom of maidenly freshness and beauty to all complexions.	Anael and Bne Seraphim
Ten o'clock	Red sandwort* opens: use this delicate plant in autumn potpourri recipes for charms to procure an abundant harvest in life and to reap the rich golden dreams of your soul.	Auriel or Uriel
Eleven o'clock	Star of Bethlehem opens: use this efficacious and blessed herb in infusions for the relief of shocks and mental distress.	Cassiel and Agiel
Twelve o'clock	Yellow goatsbeard* closes: use the golden dried heads as ingredients in charmed potpourri for health and good spirits.	Michael and Nachiel

AFTERNOON	FLOWER	RULING ANGELS
One o'clock	Pink closes.	Gabriel and Malcha Betharsisim
Two o'clock	Purple sandwort closes: use as red sandwort, see above.	Samael and Graphiel
Three o'clock	Dandelion closes.	Raphael and Tiriel
Four o'clock	Lesser bindweed closes: use this pretty meadow plant for a tisane (flowers, stem, and leaves) to relieve constipation, expel impurities, and ease the pains of fever.	Sachiel and Johphiel

* No known healing properties.

AFTERNOON	FLOWER	RULING ANGELS
Five o'clock	Cat's-ear closes.	Anael and Bne Seraphim
Six o'clock	White waterlily closes: make an infusion of the flowers and leaves and wash your face with it daily so that you may be beautiful, let the drops dry of themselves on the skin.	Auriel or Uriel
Seven o'clock	Red poppy closes.	Cassiel and Agiel
Eight o'clock	Wild succory closes: make a tisane from the leaves, flowers, and roots to encourage the appetite and to treat jaundice; it is good for deranged and melancholy spirits and will bring strength and purification to those who cannot cast off long lingering illnesses. Its other country name is chicory.	Mikael and Nachiel
Nine o'clock	Chickweed closes: prepare a tisane to treat stomach ulcers and all internal anger and inflammation; eat of the herb in your salads for the iron it contains, and to aid your digestion. Wash your face with the tea, and it will shrink coarsened pores and restore or perpetuate your youthfulness of visage.	Gabriel and Malcha Betharsisim
Ten o'clock	Common nipplewort closes: use the young leaves of this plant in salads to promote purity of the system; its little yellow florets should be used in charmed potpourri recipes for lulling and soothing little restless ones into sleep; it will help your spell to work, especially when the child is ill and fractious.	Samael and Graphiel
Eleven o'clock	Sowthistle closes	Raphael and Tiriel

AFTERNOON	FLOWER	RULING ANGELS
Twelve o'clock	Mallow closes: this plant is excellent for all respiratory disorders—bronchitis, asthma, pneumonia, etc.; make a cold infusion in every case. It will soothe a sore throat and bring back the voice in cases of laryngitis, ease digestive complaints, toothache, and drive away gonorrhea with its gentle purifying qualities, which are never harsh but always effective.	Sachiel and Johphiel

This completes Flora's Dial and the table of the Angels of the Hours.

WITCH'S GARDEN

The Herb of the Virgin

Yarrow is called the herb of the Virgin because it is a woman's herb and a witch's herb, rich in its efficacious power in magic and incantations. Look for the yarrow in the wild and carry home its seeds. You will find it flowering in the early summer, in the meadows and the pastures, and on farmers' land lying fallow. Its leaves are of a dark, gray-greenish hue, like curling feathers of lace, and if you crush them gently, their aroma will rise and suggest to your senses the twilight magic of nature under a full moon and the deep olive-green of the forces of life as they move in majesty through the earth. These things the witches knew of old, and any wort-cunning or spellmaking that allied itself with the powers of darkness they knew they could ward off with this mystic herb of the Virgin.

The flowers of the yarrow, which continue into September and even beyond (if the autumn brings a Saint's Summer or Indian Summer), are little things, white but washed with a tinge of pink or delicate lilac. They grow in umbels, clustered like tiddy daisies.* They have a sharp scent that foxes are said to like.

The yarrow needs a hot, sunny spot, and it likes a well-drained, dry soil. You may gather its leaves and its flowers all summer long, but if you wish to dry the herb, take what you need of it in the early summer. If you hear that a wedding is to take place, give a sprig of the Virgin's herb to the bride, for that is lucky for both. It will bring her seven years of married happiness, and if you bless the herb with a witch's charm, her blissful years will number seven times seven.

Make a tisane, and minister it for chills, colds, fever, twinges in the ear, eczema, diarrhea, and headaches. An ointment from its leaves and flowers (you must use both in the tisane also) will heal wounds. Take the yarrow tea as a tonic for debility or convalescence. It will soothe measles, chicken pox, small pox, Bright's disease, and diabetes. It will cleanse and soothe the stomach and take away indigestion and palpitations.

Women particularly should drink an infusion of the yarrow from time to time to keep them free from feminine troubles. It will steady or encourage the menstrual flow as needed. Inflammation of the ovaries, prolapse of the uterus, and fibroids are helped by drinking two cups of the tea daily and by taking yarrow baths. Even cancers of the stomach have been cured in this way.

The tea is also known to help rheumatic pains, liver and kidney disorders, diseases of the bone marrow, and ailments of

* Tiddy is a country word meaning between small and tiny.

the circulatory system. It will ease weakness and pain in the heart and chase away constipation.

Yarrow is a Venus herb. Like the Virgin, it is full of grace and a cure for all ills. Use it to bring great blessing and potency to your magics and spells.

Yarrow is the emblem of mother love, and in the Language of Lovers it says, "Be comforted, for love is the salve of all sorrows."

Chapter Seven

SEPTEMBER

The Nut-Brown Maiden

God's Grandeur

The world is charged with the grandeur of God.
It will flame out, like shining from shook foil;
It gathers to a greatness, like the ooze of oil
Crushed. Why do men then not now reck his rod?
Generations have trod, have trod, have trod;
And all is seared with trade; bleared, smeared with toil;
And wears man's smudge and shares man's smell; the soil
Is bare now, nor can foot feel, being shod.

And for all this, nature is never spent;
There lives the dearest freshness deep down things;
And though the last lights off the black West went
Oh, morning, at the brown brink eastward, springs—
Because the Holy Ghost over the bent
World broods with warm breast and with ah! bright wings.

Gerard Manley Hopkins

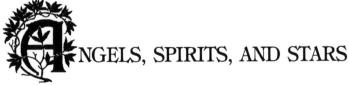

ANGELS, SPIRITS, AND STARS

Libra is usually considered remarkable as the one inanimate sign of the zodiac, and from medieval times onward it has been represented simply as a pair of scales. Earlier sigils for this sign, however, depict a woman who is holding the scales forward in her right hand, while her left hand points to them and also to her heart. This archetypal woman surely demonstrates, in symbolic form, the esoteric concept that it is Woman, the Spirit of Wisdom, who will convey the spiritual message and impetus that will eventually lead the sexes to a state of harmony and equality; this, in turn, will endow humankind with the conditions it needs to take a gargantuan and wholly unprecedented forward leap in its evolution.

According to tradition, the scales of Libra were portrayed in the claws of Scorpio, so that the two signs were one (sometimes Libra was called "chelae" or "the claws of the scorpion"). This would further indicate such an esoteric teaching, as Scorpio is the sign of sexuality and death and has rulership over the organs of generation, suggesting the Buddhist Wheel of life and death, the birth and death and rebirth cycle of matter and the earth that is under the care and dominion of the goddess or the Great Mother. The sting of death is in the scorpion's tail, and her claws represent the pincer-squeeze of life's sufferings, frustrations, agonies and limitations as we meet the challenges of the earth plane and its physical matter which is our thralldom; but the eternal promise is in the loving smile of the Goddess as she sits spinning the wheel. Humanity *will* triumph and release itself from the cruel grasp of Scorpio. How shall this be achieved? Only by the attain- ment of equilibrium, perfect spiritual harmony that will flow forth from transcendant humanity as a great light and bless and embrace all the earth ... and so, as is right, Libra separates itself from the Virgin, to its left, and Hecate the Scorpion, to its right, and emerges as the Child of Light, the very fulcrum of the zodiac, its point of balance.

It is noteworthy that the astrologer Ebenezer Sibly, in the horoscope he cast for Jesus Christ, gives a Libran ascendant. The ascendant is the true mate of the sun sign in any horoscope and its significance suggests the task and life purpose of the native, thus conferring on the holy Nazarene the great labor by which humanity was to be shown that the meeting-place of the divine lifeforces was its own self, and that every man and woman must tread the path that leads to inner equilibrium, following Christ on his cross-burdened way, so that the pains of sacri- fice might be transmuted into the unbounded joy of love. Thus the positive and negative forces (Virgo and Scorpio) are balanced in the heart of humankind (the heart is the center according to the mystery teachings), and the light shines forth.

To illustrate this final destiny, the zodiacal sign of Libra is depicted as a pair of scales upon which is mounted a circle at whose heart sits a god. The ancient Egyptian equivalent of *Libra* means "place of sunrise," and it is thought that the Egyptian god of Libra is thus revealed as the solar godhead. The Egyptians were renowned prophets (the Great Pyramids seem to be a huge divinatory system on a planetary and cosmic scale), and what seems to link this ancient solar deity with the Christ (called the "Light of the World") is that the Egyptian hiero-glyphic for the original Libran sign describes an image of the sun setting over the earth, suggesting not only the general location of Christianity as the religion of the Occident (symbolized by the westering sun) but also Christ as the divine Alpha and Omega. As the place of sunrise and then the sunset, Libra is the beginning and the end of the everlasting circle precisely because it is the point of balance; since this is so, the solar disc can come into full manifestation. The circle is not broken because equilibrium has been achieved. The beginning is the end, is the beginning, and shall be evermore. Eternity is achieved.

How does this "sunset" hieroglyphic demonstrate that the balance in the heart is created by harmony between the masculine and feminine spiritual principles? It would seem that the horizontal earth and the sinking sun form a cross, so that their influences run into one another. Their union creates an energy flow so that the horizontal is the vertical and vice versa. They are no longer in conflict, no longer a duality; yet although this is the deeper reality, there is a space of air, of infinite possibility, between the earth and the Sun. It is this that is the special domain of Libra, the Child of Light, for his domicile enables Libra to be the agent of union, the mediator between sun and earth (male and female), initiating relationships and harmonies, so that the two function as one.

In the role of integrating child, it is not surprising that Libra's planetary ruler is Venus, emblem of the goddess in her warm, gentle, fruitful, charming aspects. . . and so Librans are typically gentle, sensi-tive, responsive, peace loving and refined, intelligent, warm and affec-tionate, elegant and agile, particularly in mental spheres, because it is

these that air represents. This inner, airy, spiritual space that is emphasized by the sunset hieroglyph has a natural potential to inspire the
unity that is the secret of equilibrium, for everything upon the earth
breathes the same air—trees, flowers, birds, animals, insects, humanity—
even the very stones, if we can believe, as some do, that they breathe
and have a heartbeat perceptible to those who can penetrate the inner
planes.

This potential of relationship is the essence of life to Libra (and
other air signs), so interaction and communication are stressed in this
sign, as is tolerance and a sense of community. As far as Libra is
concerned, interchangeability does not have to conflict with its natural
sense of order—in fact, interchangeability *is* order. Change is the
immutable law and the true stabilizer. This view that principles must
go through the purifying fires of refinement and progress, adjustment
and tuning is a Libran and airy ideal and promotes brotherhood based
on understanding.* Librans grasp as essential and substantial that which
seems to be nonvital airy abstraction to other signs.

If Librans become unbalanced, they can lose their grip and become
impractical, falsely idealistic, and abortively intellectual, in that their
mental processes can divorce them from earthly reality. The delicacy
and refinement of Venus can manifest as languid idleness and passivity.
If this happens, it is helpful for them to remember that their great aim
is control and poise, the major lessons of the air dispensation.

odiac

LIBRA—SCALES
SEPTEMBER 23–OCTOBER 22

ANGEL: Anael
RULING PLANET: Venus
KEYWORD: Partners
AGE: 14–21 years (adolescence)

* I use the word *brotherhood* without reference to gender to denote spiritual harmony.

METAL: Copper

CROSS: Cardinal

ELEMENT: Air

QUALITIES: Harmony, gentleness, stability, discrimination, beauty, affection, partnership, marriage, social awareness, justice

ILLNESSES TO GUARD AGAINST: kidney stones, sciatica, eczema, skin eruptions, Bright's disease, nephritis, lumbago, worry, overstrained nerves

BODY AREAS: Kidneys, lumbar regions, skin

STONES: Opal, lapis lazuli, emerald, beryl, jade, turquoise, sapphire

NUMBER: 6

DAY: Friday

FLOWERS AND HERBS: Violet, white rose, love-in-a-mist

TREES: Almond, walnut, plum, myrtle, apple (especially blossoms)

ANIMALS: Hart, hare

BIRDS: Dove, swan, sparrow

COLORS: Royal blue, cerulean blue, rose-pink, amethyst, violet

In ancient Egypt *Libra* was *Ta-Akhet*, "place of sunrise," its sigil depicting a sunset. The Greeks gave it several names, one of which was "weight," or, in ancient Sicilian Greek, *Libra*.

Meditation on the Star of the Aquarian Age

The seers of our time have given us the six-pointed star as a meditation symbol for the Aquarian age, which we are now entering. The ancient mystery schools understood that the star with its six points was an emblem of the individual man or woman firmly based upon the earth and aspiring to heavenly consciousness; so it is that the undivided star (formed from the intersection of two equilateral triangles, the upward-pointing one representing our earthly self, and the downward-pointing one, the god-consciousness or god-self which descends in an embrace of brilliant illumination whenever we "sound the note" by reaching consciously upward into the spiritual spheres) is a symbol of humanity perfected—woman and man made divine.

To meditate upon the star, stand comfortably with spine erect and relaxed, perhaps near an open window, and begin to focus on your breathing. Think of your heart-center and the little flame burning there.

See this point of light within your own heart grow until it connects with the larger six-pointed star, shining above your head in the spiritual skies. Breathe in the light that pours forth from the star, and soon, on the out-breath, you will feel able to consciously direct these magical shafts of golden white light flooding from the heart of the star, and from its six points, out into the world of suffering and despairing humanity—where they will bring succor and comfort, healing and renewal, and a cleansing of unhappy conditions. Remember always that within the star are the forms of the great angels of love, of wisdom, and of power; and that these radiant angelic beings can be called upon at any time to assist us in living our lives.

Meditate upon the star at any hour—although the hours of three, six, nine, and especially twelve noon, are particularly efficacious for sending out the light in blessing (which will also confer a blessing upon yourself).

Stars of Autumn

On fine autumn nights the air is cool and still, the skies are calm and clear, and the canopy of stars in the heavens shines with a glittering brilliance very different from the soft, misty, faraway radiance of the summer stars. In September and October, look for the Milky Way, which is more distinct in this season than in any other. If you are suffering from a preponderance of earthly heaviness, there is no better cure than to go outside and view this magical river of stars sailing in the pearly mists of the Milky Way, said to have been brought into being when the child Hercules suckled the breasts of the celestial goddess Hera with such vigor that the nourishing milk formed the Milky Way; some drops also fell to earth and became the white lilies of the valleys and meadows.

Following the course of the Milky Way, Cygnus (the Swan) appears in one of its most radiant regions. Look to the left of the Lyre, and you will see a cross so distinct that it has been named the Northern Cross. A star marks its center, while three stars form its horizontal arm and four its perpendicular. A further bright star, completing the constellation, is not included in the cruciform star-glyph. The star at the heart of the Swan is the central star of a beautiful region, the last in a curving crown of stars. Deneb or Hen's Tail (the star Alpha Cygni) shines near the small rift in the Milky Way (an area where dark obscuring clouds appear to interrupt it). The great rift beginning in the Swan seems to divide the Milky Way in two; it is in Cygnus that (with the aid of a telescope) the wonderful Bridal Veil nebula can be seen.

Beta Cygni, the Swan's second star, is also called Albireo and is a double star of marvelous beauty, one of its partners shining sapphire-blue, while the other glows topaz-yellow.

DICTIONARY OF COMMON HERBS

Agrimony *(Agrimonia eupatoria)* for dry coughs, inflammation of the mouth and throat, rheumatism, lumbago, digestive trouble, spleen disorders, cirrhosis of the liver, enlargement of the heart, stomach, and lungs, kidney and bladder ailments, varicose veins and sores; agrimony soothes and restores the voice.

Angelica *(Angelica officinalis)* for tonsilitis, sore throats, flatulence, colic, and heartburn.

Balm *(Melissa officinalis)* for female disorders (in particular, infertility and menstrual irregularity), nervous ailments, hysteria.

Barley *(Hordeum pratense)* for shattered nerves, bladder and kidney diseases, general tonic.

Basil *(Ocimum basilicum)* for vomiting and nausea (especially morning and travel sickness).

Chamomile *(Anthemis nobilis)* for tumors, ulcers, intestinal worms, exhaustion, nightmares, nervous disorders; chamomile is used as a face wash, a hair lightener, and a tonic.

Cowslip *(Primula veris)* for insomnia, nervous disorders, gout, rheumatism, bladder stones, kidneys, migraine and headaches, inflammation of the heart muscle, dropsy, strokes; cowslip is a blood cleanser, and its leaves in a cold cream or jelly base will rejuvenate and refresh the complexion.

Dandelion *(Taraxacum officinale)* for disorders of the liver and the gall bladder, diabetes, rashes, itching skin, eczema, metabolic disturbances, gout, rheumatism, glandular swellings, jaundice, spleen disorders, acne, circulatory problems.

Eyebright *(Euphrasia officinalis)* for deteriorating vision, disorders of the spleen, stomach, and gall bladder, digestive disorders.

Fennel *(Foeniculum officinale)* for arthritis, cramps, gastric ailments, exhaustion, low immunity levels, poor memory, recovery from strokes, constipation, obesity.

Feverfew *(Matricaria parthenium)* for general debility, depression, confusion, headaches, poor appetite, infertility, tendency to abort, digestive problems; feverfew is often referred to as a "woman's herb," as it assists in labor and the expelling of the afterbirth.

Goldenrod *(Solidago virgaurea)* for bleeding of the intestines, disorders of the kidneys, bladder complaints, severe emotional stress, serious shocks, nervous breakdowns.

Hawthorn *(Crataegus oxycantha)* for strengthening and healing the heart, softening arteries, dizziness, palpitations, sore throats, nervous disorders.

Horsetail *(Equisetum arvense)* for purification and stimulation of the blood, disorders of the liver, kidney and gall bladder, jaundice, bladder problems, hemorrhoids, tinnitis, skin disorders, persistent herpes, pyelitis, hemorrhaging, dropsy, nerves, depression, insanity, hysteria, bronchitis.

Ivy *(Hedera helix)*—five leaves only infused in half a liter of water—for swollen glands, fevers, dropsy; no more than one tablespoon three times daily to be taken.

Knapweed *(Centaurea nigra)* for glandular disorders, catarrh, poor appetite, general debility.

Lavender *(Lavandulae Labiatae)* for nervous problems, headaches, coughs, halitosis, exhaustion, inflammation, aching muscles; lavender mouthwash strengthens the gums and firms the teeth.

Lily of the valley *(Convallaria majalis)* for the treatment of strokes, nervous ailments, high blood pressure, dropsy, insomnia.

Mallow *(Malva vulgaris)* for all internal inflammation, gastritis, ulcers, bronchitis, coughs, laryngitis, tonsilitis, dry mouth, cancer of the larynx; externally, mallow tea or ointment is used to heal wounds, ulcers, swollen feet and hands, fractures, and phlebitis.

Mistletoe *(Viscum album)* for epilepsy, chronic cramps and hysterical complaints, chilblains, diabetes, metabolic disorders, hormonal imbalance, bleeding, stroke, hardening of the arteries, visual defects, heart and circulatory disorders, dizziness, tinnitis, fatigue, apathy, high blood pressure, femine disorders, cancer.

Nettle *(Urtica dioica)* for eczema, headaches, disorders of the bladder and urinary passage, constipation, cancer, viral diseases, liver, gall bladder and spleen disorders, congestion of the lungs, fatigue, ageing, dropsy, allergies, blood disorders, sciatica, lumbago, neuritis, gout, rheumatism, depression, nervous disorders, weariness.

Oak *(Quercus robur)* (young bark and leaves) for internal hemorrhaging, "flooding" during menstruation, internal and external cleanliness; the tisane will heal damaged tissue in the stomach and intestines.

Parsley *(Petroselinum sativum)* for halitosis, diseases of the bladder and kidneys, arthritis, sciatica, jaundice; parsley is a tonic and a purifier for the urinary system.

Plantain *(Plantago lanceolata)* for disorders of the respiratory system, especially bronchitis, asthma, whooping cough, and tuberculosis, bladder disorders, stings, dog bites, snake bites, thrombosis, glandular disorder; crushed, fresh leaves will treat malignant growths.

Red clover *(Trifolium pratense)* for headache, neuralgia, nausea, cancer (preventive), gastric disorders, glandular diseases, ulcers; in all cases, use the flowers only and eat a dozen or more (fresh) each day.

Rose (wild) *(Rosa Canina)* for heart and brain diseases (especially strokes), catarrh, female disorders, stomach disorders, dog bites, malaise, panacea for all ills.

Rosemary *(Rosmarinus officinalis)* for heart and liver disorders, high blood pressure, coughs, colds, influenza, nervous disorders, fatigue, digestive complaints, menstrual cramps, insomnia; the perfume of rosemary is healing in itself, and as a face wash and a shampoo it has notable beautifying effects.

Rue *(Ruta graveolens)* for mental and nervous disorders, circulatory problems, cramps, sciatica, rheumatism, glandular and arterial diseases (use the tisane sparingly—keep it light in color).

Sage *(Salvia officinalis)* for liver, bilious and digestive complaints, coughs, colds, influenza, headaches and fevers, sore throats, tender gums, poor memory, insanity, nervous complaints; sage ointment will heal skin disorders, sores, and ulcers, and will arrest bleeding and swelling.

St. John's wort *(Hypericum perforatum)* for hemorrhages, neuritis, nervous disorders, insomnia, hysteria, depressions, sleep walking, glandular complaints; the ointment is healing for all wounds, sciatica, sunburn, rheumatism.

Thistle *(Cirsium vulgare)* for liver disorders and impurities of the blood, circulatory problems, malaise, low spirits, depression, heart, brain, and kidney complaints, impaired memory.

Thyme *(Thymus serpyllum* [wild], *Thymus vulgaris* [garden]) for digestive problems, fevers, liver disorders, epilepsy, insanity, psychological illness, headaches, halitosis, hysteria, female disorders, malaise, fatigue.

Valerian *(Valeriana officinalis)* for nervous complaints, depression, insomnia (use a decoction from the root or the fresh juice—one tablespoon or one teaspoon, respectively, each day; use sparingly).

Violet *(Viola odorata, Viola canina)* for stones and gravel in the bladder, nervous complaints, mental sluggishness, pleurisy, chest and lung complaints, heart problems, angina pectoris, headaches; swollen glands, skin eruptions, tumors, and bruises benefit from a combination of internal treatment (violet tisane) and violet ointment applied externally.

Wood sorrel *(Oxalis acetosella)* for liver and blood disorders, kidney and bladder complaints, diseases of the genital glands.

Yarrow *(Achillea millefolium)* for colds, fevers, headaches, influenza, diarrhea, palpitations, female disorders, abdominal disorders, prolapse of the uterus, fibroids, neuritis, migraine, bone marrow disorders, rheumatic and back pain, constipation; for women, yarrow is a panacea.

WISEWOMAN'S JOURNAL

Advice for the Herb Healer

GATHERING HERBS

Gather your herbs in a basket; a wide, flat one is better than a deep, small one. When a sickness is severe, it is important to use fresh herbs to treat it. Once gathered, the sooner they are brewing in the pot and being administered to the patient, the better. If you find it impracticable to seek out the herbs in the wild so that they may come fresh to the pot every day, you may gather enough to last a few days. Lay them out in your basket and take care not to crush them. At home, let them lie on fresh clean paper or cloth, only very daintily covered, in a cool place in the pantry. In cases in which the illness to be treated is advanced and morbid, fresh herbs daily are often the only chance of effecting a complete recovery. When the ailment is not so serious or life threatening, dried herbs may be given.

When you gather from the wilderness, you must know your herbs so well that there cannot be a mistake. It is not always easy to learn from books. Find an expert who will befriend you and enlighten your perplexities. If you are earnest in your endeavors, especially when you intend to help others, the right help will come. Do not doubt my words, but believe in them, for faith is the key. When you sincerely wish to use the herbs of the earth for your health and happiness, you are reaching out to the goddess, and she cannot help but hear you. Therefore, do not be discouraged if at first the help you need does not come, for come it will in due course.

You may pick fresh herbs from the earliest stirrings of the spring until the end of November. There are some, like rosemary, that you can gather virtually all year round. When you gather herbs for drying, there are times and seasons to be observed so that the plants you pick will be especially rich in their god-given properties. Roots are best extracted in the early spring or during the autumn. Leaves may be taken before and during the time of flowering. When it is the flowers you need, take them just as the herb's flowering season begins. Fruits should be collected as they are beginning fully to ripen.

It is better to gather herbs, for drying or otherwise, on a fine sunny day, in the morning when the dew has gone, or at noon, when the volatile oils are most active. If you cannot gather at these times, remember the plants are still valuable, even though their healing properties are not quite so marked or vigorous. In all circumstances, take only strong and healthy plants that are not infested with blight or pests. Pick your leaves and flowers carefully, talking to the plant all the while, even if only in your mind. Never pull up a plant unless you need its roots. You must convey to the little living creature that you need the blessing of its leaves and flowers for your healing work, or, if they are for you, for your sickness. In your heart, ask the fairies which stems you should take. They will show you how to avoid hurting the plant, how to take from it so that it will continue to grow with vigour. They will tell you when you have taken enough from one plant, and must move on to another, or, if you have not yet learned how to talk to the nature spirits, another kindly guide will help you, or yet perhaps an angel.

Author's Note

Under present-day conditions, it is important not to gather herbs that grow along busy roadsides where they are continually saturated in toxic fumes, and to be careful of the banks of heavily polluted rivers or waterways, and of industrial sites and busy railway embankments. If fields are sprayed with pesticides and fertilizers that are not organic, don't stray close to their edges when gathering, and avoid using plants growing among the crop. When picking, use an "herb basket'," as advised, certainly never a plastic container.

DRYING

I have known those who wash their herbs heartily before drying, even leaving them to soak "clean" in bowls. Remember, as soon as you flush your herbs with water, their virtues begin to wash away. Therefore, let the merest sprinkle and a good shake do the job, or, better still, if you know your gathering spot is clean, do not wash them at all.

Spread your herbs in thin layers on cloth or clean paper (not newspaper). They must be dried quickly in warm, airy, shaded rooms. If you have a still-room or an attic, this would serve excellently. Dry roots and bark (and thick-stemmed herbs) in a warm oven, keeping the temperature even and low.* Roots and bark, of course, have to be washed well before drying. Test your herbs for dryness by bending them. If they are brittle and snap, then the job is done. Put them in green glass jars (to keep off the sun) or, if you have only plain glass, put them in a cupboard. Do not keep them forever. When spring comes, clear them out and gather a fresh harvest. Herbs lose their properties over time.

OILS

Take two ounces of the herb you have chosen, and crush and pound it to refinement, using a mortar and pestle. Now take

* Not more than 35°C (95°F).

eight fluid ounces of corn oil or almond oil (you may use castor but not olive; it goes rancid in time) and one good tablespoon of cider vinegar. Put your herbs in a glass jar, pour in the oil and the vinegar, and leave in a warm place in your still-room, or somewhere in the sun, for two weeks. Strain the mixture through muslin, squeeze the residue of oil out of the herbs and add it to your compound, then throw the herbs away and start all over again, adding fresh herbs to your infant oil until it smells as sharp and fragrant as pleases you. Tarragon, fennel, rosemary, lavender, and yarrow are good, but try as many different recipes as you wish. You will have to be patient if you wish to prepare a rose oil, for the fragrance of the rose is so subtle and delicate that the oil has to be processed many, many times.

If it is your desire to prepare a magical oil (and what better way is there to add blessings to it?), then you must gather the herbs for your oil at the appropriate angelic hour and day and prepare it similarly; but remember that it is the outpouring of your own soul and the light in your heart that are the most potent forces in your magic. Observe the tides of the moon so that you begin, if you can, when the moon is new (Bride's moon). Bear in mind that the new moon's horns point toward the east, as though it is the sun newly risen, while the old moon's horns point to the west.

Author's Note

If no mortar and pestle is available, a blender will do. When making up the magical oils, however, your own sweat and tears will add to their efficacy. Appropriate classical music helps, too; strict silence must be observed except for that stimulus, however—except, of course, if you are using charms.

Tisanes

Snip the fresh herbs to the required quantity, which will usually be two teaspoonsful, or a palmful, whichever you like; put in the pot (your own special herb teapot, which must never be used for any other purpose than brewing herbal teas and which should always be earthenware or china, never pewter or any other metal). Bring two cupfuls of water to the boil and pour over the herbs. Leave to brew for just under one minute, no longer. If you are using dried herbs, leave for a little longer, but no more than two minutes. The tea should be a sparkling lime color, or pale lemon, never cloudy or muddy in its appearance. If you are using roots, put them in the water, bring to the boil, take off the heat, and allow them to soak for three minutes. Then you may drink the infusion. Sip one cupful in the morning, one throughout the day, then make up another cupful for the evening. Generally this will prove enough, but if you or your patient is very ill, the tea must be taken in considerable quantities. Only in this way will the disease be driven back until it gives quarter.

Some herbs need to be infused in cold water. In that case, put the herbs in cold water overnight, and take out in the morning. The tisane may then be drunk, but if the patient prefers it warm (it cannot be hot), then heat it very slightly until the chill is taken off. If any healing herb does not seem to be working for the patient, before you substitute another just try a mixture of the hot and cold tisanes. Soak the herbs in only half of the full amount of water you need for the prescribed tisane, overnight as usual, take out the herbs in the morning, then pour the rest of the water needed for the tea over the discarded herbs; throw the herbs away and mix the cold and the hot infusions to make up the required amount.

(If you have a heart problem, be careful of taking vast quantities of fluid, and include a diuretic herb* in your treatment.)

JUICES

Squeeze out the juice from the fresh herb with your fingers or crush the herb with a rolling pin. Let it drop into little bottles and seal them well. In a cool room they will keep for a week or two, but they are better prepared fresh every two days.

---

* The fresh leaves of the dandelion are best, together with the milk from the hollow stems (drink purified water to ease the taste as you dose yourself).

They are to be taken as medicinal drops or applied straight on to the flesh, as required.

TINCTURES

Take three ounces of the required herb, put them in a container, and pour over them a quart of corn spirits (rye whiskey or vodka). Surgical spirits (rubbing alcohol) will do if you have no wish to use the tincture as an internal medicine; it can be rubbed in as a massage or put directly on to the affected parts. Seal well, and put it to stand in a very warm spot for three weeks. You must give the bottle a hearty shake twice a day. Then strain away the herbs, wringing them out to obtain as much moisture as possible. Keep the bottled tincture away from sunlight once the process is completed.

FRESH OINTMENT

Crush the stems, leaves, and flowers, spread a clean piece of cloth with the pulp, and put straight on to the body, binding round with a bandage to keep in place. Keep on as long as possible (but not more than twelve hours, when the process is repeated).

HERBAL POULTICE

Macerate the herbs, heat them to a comfortable temperature in the oven, put them straight on to the naked skin, and hold them there with a tight binding of linen.

OINTMENT

Warm petroleum jelly, stirring in a little honey. Pound four handfuls of the required chopped herb in your mortar and pestle, gradually adding the herbs to the jelly as you go (you will need a big jar of jelly to accommodate all the herbs). Then warm through again, put into pots, and leave to gel.

HERBAL BATHS

Use one bucketful of herbs or six ounces of dried herbs. Let them soak overnight in cold water, heat and strain, and pour straight into the bath. Stay in the bath, keeping it warm, for half an hour. On emerging, keep well wrapped up in towels, and let the water dry on your skin.*

POTPOURRRI

Gather the leaves, flowers, berries, seeds, and stems of your choice in the usual way (in the morning on a sunny day, the leaves to be picked just before the plant flowers) and dry them thoroughly. Big-petaled flowers need to have their petals stripped, so they may be dried separately. Put into airtight jars with two ounces of orris root, three ounces of ground calamus root, and two good tablespoons of sea salt. Put in cloves, cinnamon, and nutmeg, dried lemon peel, and a touch of ginger, too, so that your recipes will have an undertow of the spiced breezes of the world in their perfume. Leave in a dark cupboard until you are ready to make up individual scents and charmed fragrances. When it is your wish to concoct magical potpourri, observe the angelic days and hours, the tides of the moon, and the signs of the zodiac, as well as blessing the flowers and your work with runes and spells, in the usual way. Always remember that your imagination, the power of your dreams, and the visions of your heart are your three great magical tools.

Blessings on your herb-healing and spell-working, and on all the facets of your craft.

---

* These instructions are given for medicinal baths only; it is not necessary to follow them when taking herb beauty baths or revitalizing baths.

WISEWOMAN'S WEATHERBOOK

The spider can tell the weather; when you see her busy spinning her web, be assured that fine weather is coming to stay awhile; and if she changes her web between six and seven of the clock in the evening, expect a still and fine night.

When house martins scream and swoop about your house in great numbers, and especially if they nest in the eaves, it is a sure sign of a long and glorious summer; if they are scarce, expect a summer of drenching rains when the angels are busy washing clean the finer ethers; when they are pure and shining, we may generally look forward to an All Hallows or Saint's Summer to cheer our spirits and shorten the winter.

When the scent of flowers from the garden hangs sweet and heavy in the air as though you took a nosegay about with you, and their perfume steals in at your open doorway smelling more voluptuous and magical even than evening-scented blooms, you can be sure of rain sweeping in from the west before very long.

Search among the grasses of a meadow for clover leaves; if these be drawn closely together as if in prayer, thunder and rain is coming on; and if you pop a leaf into your shoe, you'll find the fairies and dance with them before the moon comes up, if you're diligent enough carefully to watch and wait through the turning of no less than three hours.

Chapter Eight

OCTOBER

The Stirring of the Old Gods

This Ae Nighte

This ae nighte, this ae nighte,
Every nighte and alle,
Fire and fleet and candle-lighte,
And Christe receive thy saule.

When thou from hence away art past,
—Every nighte and alle,
To Whinny-muir thou com'st at last;
And Christe receive thy saule.

From Whinny-muir when thou mayst pass,
Every nighte and alle,
To Brig o' Dread thou com'st at last;
And Christe receive thy saule.

From the "Lyke-Wake Dirge"

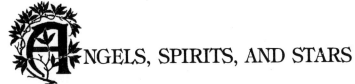

ANGELS, SPIRITS, AND STARS

The Celtic New Year, Samhain, fell on November 1 in the old round of the year. It is no mystery, then, to find that the sign of Scorpio signifies death; for in the northern hemisphere, the year is dying when the sun is in Scorpio, the angel of the year is departing, there is a release from form as the trees shed their leaves and the herbs, flowers, and grasses wither. Fiery Mars, one of the ruling planets of Scorpio, seems himself to wield the death blow as his red, orange, vermilion, and gold hues burn everywhere in the falling and decaying foliage; yet, as the frosts come and we see the subtle spirits of the dead herbs and flowers of summer cling in delicate and beautiful companies of ghosts in the morning frosts on the windowpane, it is not difficult to make a connection between Mars the warrior and Mars the healer; for Mars is releasing the spirit everywhere, sacrificing the mortal body so that the soul may soar heavenward, no longer a prisoner of the dull clay.

Within the Scorpio constellation shines the great star Antares, or anti-Mars; the firmament itself states that Mars must play a dual role, must look in the mirror, become a reversal of himself, and so find his profoundest depths. It is said that when the scorpion is ringed round with fire, it will sting itself to death; this is the spirit of Mars in Scorpio. He will open the deepest wounds in himself to find new possibilities, even though they spell his death. He will end life to begin it. His arid dance of death creates a desert of the world, and yet the claws of the scorpion, the claws of duality, grasp the Libran Venus. With his lover, death may be overcome and the great rebirth initiated, for Venus is both evening and morning star.

And so there are two sigils for Scorpio; one is the desert creature, depicted so that it greatly resembles the severed tail of the dragon, symbol of the undifferentiated power of the physical and earthly life that has to be absorbed into the flame of the spirit so that it may no more cause death, suffering and destructive darkness and yet still preserve its vitality and wisdom. The other is the eagle, symbol of the sun, spiritual messenger who can gaze steadily into the blazing glory of the solar disc and fly there without harm.

The scorpionic sigil represents male and female genitalia, and certainly it is through the medium of sex that the depths of duality in the fiery, vital dragon are made known to us. Natives of this sign are fascinated by death, for they know it is the herald of regeneration. Such knowledge makes them fearless against corruption, for the advanced types can ask "Death, where is thy sting?" with true zeal, realizing that its powers cannot hold sway eternally. The sexual drive in humanity has Mars as its overlord and can be used for both creative and destructive purposes. The earliest known symbol for the zodiacal sign is the Egyptian demotic, portraying Scorpio as an erect serpent, the life forces thus awakened and vigorous, but dangerous. The earthly scorpion, the airy eagle, the fiery influence of Mars, and the assignation of water as the type of the sign itself, make Scorpio the meeting place of the four elements; these elements may appear to war—but in reality, they are struggling fiercely to achieve equilibrium.

The waters in Scorpio run deep, and could be likened to a well, ever a symbol of holiness. Wells nurture and sustain life, yet it is possible for their waters to be contaminated. The nature of a true-to-type Scorpio reflects the depth of the well, its water starred with the devotion and passion of Mars. Advanced Scorpio people have qualities that are suggested by deep well-water reflecting stars—they are inspired, shrewd, penetrating, passionate, zealous, creative, intense, confident, vigorous, commanding, and ruthless. They possess healing qualities and spiritual power, yet they can also be bitterly jealous, misanthropic, cruel, and rebellious, even criminal, weaving violent webs of deceit and intrigue. If they do this, they exchange the mysterious and beautiful Underworld over which Pluto (their other ruling planet) reigns as its ancient god, for the mundane, crude and earthly prototype beloved of the Mafia and other illicit organizations.

Pluto was discovered some sixty years ago and is the last planet in our solar system. It is small, eccentric, and mysterious. Its emanations are highly subtle, and it is believed that we have some way to advance as a species before we can truly absorb and understand its complex play upon our refined bodies. In myth, Pluto was the ruler of the dead and the Underworld, son of Saturn and brother to Neptune and Jupiter. Like his father, Pluto held dominion over the precious stones and metals of the earth—its buried treasure. His spiritual endowments were a helmet of darkness, a two-pronged scepter, and a goad with which he drove the hapless shades of the dead. He stole Persephone from the sunlit world above and made her his queen, although she divided each year equally between his shadowed domain and the upper world. Pluto's companion was Cerberus, the dog-god with three heads who devoured the souls of the unworthy.

Astrologically, Pluto imparts the qualities of duality, contradiction, transformation, and annihilation. It governs the act of sex and wealth, both powerful drives in the psyche that, if left untransformed in their mundane state, can pitilessly goad humanity to make an arid desert of the planet and their relationships with one another and the universe through a lust for power and personal domination (the discovery of Pluto coincided with the rise of Hitler, the establishment of the Mafia, and the development of the atom bomb). Pluto demonstrates that the vital dragon of duality (the earthly powers inherent in humanity) must be transformed into its higher state if it is not to wreak destruction on itself. Cancer and Scorpio share a correlation in this respect. Both bear the ominous pincers of duality. Pluto is the planet of reversal and upheaval, ensuring balance and progress in this role through the equilibrium of Libra, whose scales of justice the Scorpion grasps in its claws.

Zodiac

SCORPIO—SCORPION
OCTOBER 23–NOVEMBER 21

ANGELS: Samael and Azrael

RULING PLANETS: Mars and Pluto

KEYWORD: Death—renunciation, sacrifice, rebirth

AGE: Seniority (final stage of life)

METAL: Iron, plutonium

CROSS: Fixed

ELEMENT: Water

QUALITIES: Power, energy, intensity, will, magnetism, subtlety, resurrection, elimination, renewal, resolution

ILLNESSES TO GUARD AGAINST: All ailments of the genitals, bladder and rectum, inflammations, nervous ills, worry, mental stress

BODY AREAS: Bladder, genitals, rectum

STONES: Ruby, garnet, bloodstone, beryl, topaz, turquoise, jet

NUMBER: 9

DAY: Tuesday

FLOWERS AND HERBS: Sweet basil, lesser celandine, purple heather, chrysanthemum

TREES: Holly, blackthorn

ANIMALS: Scorpion, wolf, panther, dog, wild boar
BIRDS: Eagle, vulture, dragon, griffin, phoenix.
COLORS: Deep, dark shades of red, russet-brown, shadow-
black, stone-gray

Scorpio has twin astrological images, one depicting a scorpion or the severed tail of a serpent, its fork or claws illustrating the duality of sexuality and death, the other a resurgent eagle poised to fly into the sun.

 # editation on Pluto

Light a brown candle at midnight and dedicate it to the Archangel Azrael, whose wings bring healing and release into the light.

> Angel Azrael, help me to look into your Underworld where all secret things are, and all beauty and possibility dwell in embryonic form. I perceive the glitter and hues of precious stones as their lights illumine the restful shadows of your domain. I hear its subterranean echoes and feel its power. Here is the earth's energy-center, and my own. Help me to penetrate its depths so that I may see and learn from their profundity.

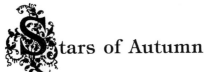 # tars of Autumn

Moving from Cygnus farther down the stream of the Milky Way, the constellation Aquila, or the Eagle, may be found. Look for its three brightest stars, which form a line, extending downward to its fourth star, which is aligned with two more pointing northwest; in the constellation's northwest corner shine two further stars; the star that completes the group is to be found at its southwestern extremity, twinkling against a backdrop of bright milky light that is known as Sobieski's Shield. Aquila's first star, Alpha Aquilae (or, in Arabic, *Altair*, which means Flying Eagle) is a powerful star of the first magnitude, glittering with a pure blue-white light.

Lying between Aquila and Cygnus is Sagitta, the Arrow, just above the line of three stars in the Eagle. Lower, and to its left, is Delphinus, the Dolphin, which contains a distinct trapezium of four stars. Above Delphinus stalks Vulpecula, the Fox, which, true to the nature of the animal it depicts, is stealthily hidden among the stars of Aquila and Cygnus, and is difficult to identify.

To the left of Sagittarius, below Aquila, stretches Capricornus, the Goat. Its brightest stars are positioned directly below Altair, considerably lower down in the heavens.

Aquarius, the Water-Bearer, is a spacious star group, reaching from the margins of Aquila above Capricorn and extending down to the horizon. On a still autumn evening when the air is lucid, a single bright star may be observed shining below Aquarius. It is Fomalhaut, a first magnitude star, the brightest luminary in the southern constellation known as the Southern Fish (Piscis Australis); the star itself is named the Fish's Mouth.

WISEWOMAN'S JOURNAL

The Hallowe'en Party

Hallowe'en is a time for merrymaking and feasting with friends, and afterward sitting up late into the night to pursue your own spiritual contemplations, your magical labors, and your communion with the saints and the spirits of those you hold dear who no longer dwell with you in the Vale of Tears.

A favorite game with young maidens is to set rows of nuts upon the bars of the grate as the fire roars and charm them thus:

> If he loves me, pop and fly;
> If he hates me, shrivel and die!

And so, in jest, they watch to see whether their sweethearts be true.

The maid who wishes to work lovespells will have collected the seeds of the butterdock (hemp or common dock may be substituted) and have kept them safe in a charm-bag until Hallowe'en, or Nutcracker Night, as it used to be known. Other maidens at the party, three, seven or nine in total they may be, must join her in walking to a secluded spot in the garden or some little further distance, where she will take out the charm-bag from her sleeve and dispense the seeds among her friends, keeping a palmful for herself. Thereafter the maids will disperse, each going to find her own place, apart from the others, to work the spell. Every maid will bow to the moon and begin to walk slowly in a ring, then three steps, a ring, then three steps, moving always to the left; she will scatter the seed and murmur this charm:

> I sow, I sow!
> Then, my own dear,
> Come here, come here,
> And mow, and mow.

She will shortly begin to make out the specter of her future husband mowing at a short distance from her as the moonlight plays upon the garden. She must take care not to tremble or swoon, as the spell is then broken, not to be essayed again until the following year.

Another lovespell may be worked in this wise: blow out the candles and open the curtains, so that the moon and the stars shine into the room where you are making your party. The hostess must choose a book and pass it to the first guest, who will ask a question of her fate, open it, and place a finger somewhere on the text. The candle is lit again, and the maid reads out nine lines according to the haphazard choice of her forefinger, in which she must read, with the help of the other guests, her fortune in love; and so is the book passed around to each guest, who performs likewise.

To reveal secrets of your future destiny, each guest must go alone with a candle to the woodpile and, with eyes tightly closed, draw therefrom promiscuously one of the faggots of wood. She will then bear it back into the house, where the party makers will help her to determine her future; if it is crooked and full of knots, she may expect some unexpected changes and perplexities through which she must pass to find happiness; if it is straight and free from knots, she will sail peacefully and uneventfully throughout life; if it is green, she will be youthful all her life long; if it is dry and wizened, she will live to a ripe old age; if an insect sits upon it, that is to be taken as money-luck; and etc., etc. This method may also be used to discover unto yourselves the kind of husband you will marry, by examining the faggot with imagination. A handsome, upright mate is prognosticated by a clean, straight piece of wood; a crabbed, sour, ill-favored fellow by a knotty and crooked piece; etc. Any maiden unduly distressed by fate's prognosis for her should bear in mind that the larger part of these party spells are to be taken in jest.

It is a merry pastime for maids to make the Hallowe'en Man, which you can burn on your bonfire the next week instead of Guy Fawkes (the Hallowe'en Man was made and burnt before Guy Fawkes). The Hallowe'en Man or Woman is your old self which you will want to cast off and burn in readiness for the New Year, which in olden times began upon the first day of November. Put pretty things upon your Hallowe'en Man or Woman and stuff him or her with a few little bags of magic herbs, placed here and there about the body, for these are of the essence of the goddess, who presides over rebirth. Put a crown upon the head, for that is the circle of the old year, and a gift from the god for you. What you have learnt in its magic ring of twelvemonths will always stay with you, for such lessons are the gold of the earth life.

When you make the Lucifer Lantern, remember that it is a turnip, because that vegetable, which grows from clay and will rot back into clay, is a symbol for our own bodies; but the rushlight or candle inside it is eternal spirit, which cannot die. The triangles you cut for the mouth, the nose, and the eyes, are sigils of our earthly self aspiring heavenwards like incense. As you cut them, intone to yourself as a charm that you will see no evil, hear no evil, and speak no evil, all the year through, and think upon the seven sacred apertures in your skull through which you perceive and take of the elixir that is life. The seven days of the week correspond to these, and the weekly cycle of the year, which is fifty-two weeks. Numerologically speaking, fifty-two is 5 + 2 which again equals seven; and the gods and angels of the inner planets are seven. All is sacred.

The Lucifer Lantern

The Lucifer Lantern, or Jack-o'-Lantern, is to be set upon the table as a centerpiece for the delight of your guests on Hallowe'en. On the next day, old New Year's Day in the Celtic tradition, you must bury it deep and bless the spot, to show your allegiance with the soil of Mother Earth, which nurtures you.

The Hallowe'en Cake

There is an old recipe for the Hallowe'en Cake, which you will find good to follow. Heat black treacle (molasses) on the stove, mixing it well with butter. You must beat them together vigorously. Pour in a generous quantity of fine oatmeal, add cinammon and cream and brown sugar and a dash of ginger. Put in a measure of best clover honey to keep it soft, then pour out into trays and leave to cool. Decorate with little sprigs of angelica and fresh blackberries. Scrub your mouth well after partaking of it, for this cake attacks the teeth. Nettle tea taken very hot, with aniseed, will take away the sweetness and wash the teeth efficaciously.

When you have done eating, and drinking, and merrymaking with your guests, and they have bidden you goodnight and gone home, then is the time for quiet reflection and spell working.

Magical Dolls
(Angel, Soul, and Guiding Spirit)

Take seven white candles and melt them down in a little crock by the heat of the fire (a metal pan must not be used). When the wax is soft and warm, test it to ensure that it does not hold too great a heat; otherwise, you will burn your fingers in the enterprise to come.

If the wax is of an even temperature, put it on the hearth to keep warm and go and fetch a phial of lavender oil and three blue candles. Light the candles and bless them, setting them near you, and rub the lavender oil well into your fingers and palms. Then take up a portion of the softened wax, which should be warm to the touch but not hot, and begin to work it into an effigy of your own self, marking it with your star sign, a secret symbol of your own, and with the sign of the cross. When you have finished approximating the little doll, lay it in a piece of clean white linen.

Now go and fetch a phial of rose oil and rub it again well into your palms and fingers after having washed off the lavender oil. You must then set to work to craft a wax doll in the shape of a spirit, which must take the form you see in your imagination. To see the gentle spirit, look into the fire, for in its slumbering depths you will espy what you seek; only remember that a spirit is like unto a human being, only more radiant and aglow with colors. When you behold the spirit in your mind's eye, put its shape into the wax, and press something bright at its heart, so that it is worn like a jewel.

Next, you must bring oil of amber, and use it in the same

way; then you will begin to fashion the third waxen figure, which is an angel with its wings spread wide to afford protection and inspiration.

There is no need to be perplexed if you cannot sculpt with skill. Should your travail result in no more than the merest approximation, the effigies will yet serve you well.

When you have done, make your own planetary sign upon the forehead of the angel, for it represents your guardian angel, who contacts you through your planet. The second figure is your spiritual guide, and the third, naturally, is yourself. Anoint all three dolls with a drop of rose oil, then wrap them up in snowy white linen and bind them with a golden thread or a golden ribbon. Put them away somewhere safe so that only you know they are there, and, whenever you are troubled or unhappy, or you have some secret of the heart to impart, you may take out your three waxen effigies and be reminded of your guide and your angel; and may you be encouraged to speak to them often, to ask for help and guidance. When you can do this continually, the spell will have gone inside you, and you will not need the little dolls anymore.

When you have cleared away (pour scalding water into the crock to clean it), you may hold communion with those beloved of you who are in spirit. It is time now for a different kind of party, for those you love will come when they hear your call. Speak to your friends; and before you go to bed, ask the spirit of the fire to leave a message for you in the ash; then, if you creep downstairs at first light, before the grate has been touched, you will find impressed within the ash a word or a sign that you will understand, so you must look sharp to be sure of not missing it; and thank the fire spirit for its grace.

Before you go to bed, you may place your shoes in such a way as to form the letter T, which is a form of the most holy cross called the Tau. It signifies the great Tree of Life upon which our Savior was hung to die and is therefore a precious and sacred symbol that will give you the means to receive an answer to your heart's deepest questions. Form the Tau with your shoes upon retiring to bed and, as you settle down for sleep, intone this rune:

> Hoping this night great visions to see
> I place my shoes in the form of a T;
> Dream-Spirit, come with soul and face fair
> So my waiting heart shall be free from all care.

Then your own Dream Spirit will come and take you out upon a great sea where you will make a voyage of discovery; and so shall the secrets of destiny be made known to you while you sleep. Have pen and paper in readiness at your bedside, for you will dream strange dreams this night, which must be treasured in memory and consulted for meaning and enlightenment long after Hallowe'en is past.

Charm to Call upon the Bargest

There is a guardian hound, a good dog, upon which you may call, should it fall upon you to have to journey home in the dark, or across a lonely stretch of the countryside; yet if you are afraid, do not be chary of summoning the bargest wherever you are, whether it be town or wilderness, as he will always come to those of good faith. Here are three rules:

1. Never demand as if you would insult the Bargest.
2. Never be churlish or ungrateful for his services. Take care to thank him.
3. Call upon him only when you genuinely need his services, never in idleness.

These rules must be acted upon in all dealings with the fairies and their spirit animals, for they will punish a person selfish or destructive and sneering in spirit. Call thus to the Bargest with this charm three times over:

Good dog, gentle hound
To my journey's end I'm bound;
I bid thee in Christ's name so pure
Walk thou with me to my door.

Guard me from harms and all foul weather
Bargest! Bargest! Come thou hither!

Soon you will see, or perhaps just hear, a great black dog padding softly behind you, bigger than a horse; or it could be that you will perceive only a shadow, or the ghost of its breath. Do not let your heart be troubled, for the Bargest is driven by an angel, and no better protection could you have in this world.

To Commune with the Spirit of a Tree

Go out into the countryside, as far as you can from streets and houses, and find a tree that your heart selects as your own. It may be that you walk straight to it, as if guided. You will sense whether the tree welcomes you or not.

Now you must name your tree, and give it a name that is noble and does it honor. Keep the name secret. The tree is your tree; you are its spiritual friend, and it will be your magical companion. A bond of love and knowledge will begin to grow between you.

Stand before your tree and let a quietude and a stillness of mind and heart fall upon you. You must place your hands upon its trunk until you feel there is a lucid language wrought in runes on its bark, a face traced in its patterns of leaf and twig, a heart within that beats in time with your own. Embrace the tree and, in your heart, bow in reverence, for the Spirit of Trees is mighty and ancient, even if your tree is young. Say to the tree:

Tree-spirit, hear my prayer
True friendship with you I would share.

If all feels well and you sense an offering of shelter and protection from the tree, you may proceed with the charm:

> Heart to heart I bind us
> Soul to soul I bind us;
> I am bound in your roots
> My soul in your fruits
> Your sap in my blood
> My breath in your wood
> My voice in your leaves
> Your strength in my griefs
> My heart in your joy . . .
>
> By magic's employ
> And spirit's wise sanction
> Let this spell be done
>
> So saith the witch.

Then tie a lock of your hair around a leafy twig and bury it deep between the roots (do not leave it upon the tree, as little birds are much annoyed by human hair, for it knots up their feet with its fine threads).

You must visit your tree often and enter into a deep soul communion with it, but do not think this can happen only when you stand beside its greenery in the summer and its good bare bones in the winter. You must think of your tree many, many times as you live your life day by day; tell him or her (you will know which it is) your joys and sorrows and the secret longings of your heart. In happiness, rejoice with your tree; in pain, put your arms around its strong trunk, and it will take the pain from you; in times of mental distress or unease, make a picture of your tree in your mind's eye; see its stillness and its gentle exhalation of peace, and breathe with your tree. Enter into its body as if you had become a tree-woman or a tree-man. So did witches in the olden days undergo vile and terrible torture in a deep sleep, which separated their pain from them.

Do all these things, and the spell will be worked. Your tree will be your heart's closest companion.

ISEWOMAN'S WEATHERBOOK

When you see the cock and his hens all flocking together under some covert in the farmer's yard, prepare to take shelter yourself, for as folk say, "The fowls can smell foul weather."

When you hear the birds chirruping loudly in the rain, sounding light of heart as if they were up to some merriment, clear lovely weather will soon cheer your spirits.

When, upon the waters of a woodland pool or a pond lying in the bosom of a meadow, you see in the morning a little ball of mist like a wandering spirit, that is the water sprite calling down the rain, and you must take care not to be caught without your bonnet; but if the ball of mist floats up to heaven, the sun has called the water sprite up to the moon to make a holiday for a little while, and no rain will be seen till he comes back down to work again.

Chapter Nine

NOVEMBER

Samhain: The Harp of Dagda

Loving Mad Tom

From the hag and hungry goblin
That into rags would rend ye
All the spirits that stand by the naked man
In the Book of Moons defend ye!
That of your five sound senses
You never be forsaken
Nor wander from yourselves with Tom
Abroad to beg your bacon.

When I short have shorn my sour face
And swigged my horny barrel
In an oaken inn I pound my skin
As a suit of gilt apparel.
The Moon's my constant Mistress,
And the lonely owl my marrow,
The flaming drake and the nightcrow make
Me music to my sorrow.

I know more than Apollo,
For oft when he lies sleeping
I see the stars at bloody wars
In the wounded welkin weeping;
The Moon embrace her shepherd

And the queen of Love her warrior,
While the first doth horn the star of morn
And the next the heavenly Farrier.

With an host of furious fancies
Whereof I am commander,
With a burning spear, and a horse of air,
To the wilderness I wander.
By a knight of ghosts and shadows
I summoned am to tourney,
Then leagues beyond the wide world's end.
Methinks it is no journey.

Anonymous

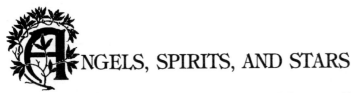# NGELS, SPIRITS, AND STARS

As the sun is reborn from the darkness, as it delivers itself from the deepest gorges of night and rises out of the terrible shadows of the Morrigan, so Sagittarius, the fiery sign of the Archer ruled by Jupiter, Sky-God Father—symbol of the inner sun of humanity's being—gloriously rises to the challenge Scorpio has set by that traverse through the cold fastnesses of the Plutonic underworld that the initiate, the disciple, the pilgrim Arjuna must undergo. And to become such a pilgrim one has to do no more than to be born a daughter or a son of the earth. Every human being is divine.

So it is that the wise Archer, his human head and embracing arms now truly emerging from the animal body of Earth ("dark Egypt," itself the Plutonic underworld) triumphantly draws his Bow (symbol of the Cross of Matter, which signifies our sojourn in the Plutonic underworld and all the lessons and deep experience we bring forth from it) and shoots an arrow skyward. That arrow is of exalted consciousness, god-consciousness, the goad of the ages as it has passed through the zodiacal archetypes. The shepherd's crook of Aries became the electrical prod of Taurus the Bull, which was, in turn, the Geminian caduceus, the huge pincers of Cancer, the downward, penetrating shaft of the Sun in Leo (in the form of an inverted triangle), the fruitful ear of corn held aloft by Virgo, the pointer of the Scales, which is also the sting of the

Scorpion (old depictions of the sign portray Libra in Scorpio's claws), the arrow of Sagittarius, which will become the panpipes of Capricornus, the Saturnian sickle of Aquarius and the rod or net wielded by Pisces, whose avatar was the Fisher of Men. (There is also a connection with the Silver Cord linking the two Fishes—see chapter 12.)

The Sagittarian arrow aims straight at the heart of the sun, becoming the eagle of St. John and his poetical Book of Revelation, for the eagle can look straight into the sun and fly to it without harm. Yet the eagle, Ethon, tore the liver from poor suffering Prometheus, bound to his rock; and it was Jupiter, ruler of Sagittarius, who commanded that this should be so. Before the eagle becomes divine and flies off into the sun, Prometheus is bound to the rock (matter) and endures the pangs of sacrifice. He has "stolen" the holy flame; it is not yet rightfully his. He must journey through the underworld of Scorpio's darkness, so that the flame, an outside, stolen thing, can penetrate inside him, to his depths; so he becomes, not the possessor of the flame, but a being who partakes consciously of its very nature. Prometheus as Sagittarius deliberately, in full consciousness, shoots his arrow. Consciousness is what the arrow symbolizes. Prometheus, at first mercilessly torn by the great claws of the eagle (the Claws of the Scorpion in their underworld guise) transfigures the horror of the bird of prey into the magnificent spiritual messenger it truly is. And, of course, Prometheus is Mercury, Messenger of the Gods, in a different guise. Prometheus himself is magically reborn, according to the promise of Scorpio, and becomes the eagle—the messenger. And so it is that St. John becomes Mercury or Prometheus, bringing to us his Revelation as receiver of the divine flame, whose mystery and beauty are more concerned with spiritual experience—as the soul is initiated into inner realms and washed with baptismal waters from the source of the spirit—rather than with dreary prophecies of doom and the end of the earth.

The sun or star at which the Archer shoots his arrow is represented in the physical universe by the bright golden star Al Nasl (the Point). The themes of Sagittarius are education and wisdom, since, in the framework of its cosmic significance, Sagittarius celebrates the tuning and refining of the lower self so that it becomes a perfect and beautiful vehicle for spirit. The Archer is half horse, half man. In a way, he is a unicorn, for the horse signifies intelligence and nobility, and the arrow that is aligned with the heart of the centaur is a manifestation of his exalted, purified intelligence. Sagittarius has found the seed of the spirit germinating in the physical. There is union of body and spirit, a yogic dance that celebrates life in the full knowledge that Matter is also Spirit. A healing takes place by which the connection between Mercury and Jupiter (both winged gods) is again emphasized, for Merlin or Raphael, Mercury's angel, bears healing in his wings.

And so Sagittarius is concerned with the refinement of education as a healing source of the undifferentiated animal nature of humanity—a means by which it may become harmonized. Teaching, lecturing, writing, the arts, organized sports, the dispensing of justice are linked with this sign. Like Mercury, Jupiter rules communication, travel, adventure, and the pioneering spirit. He gives Sagittarian people a longing for freedom—sometimes at too high a cost. Yet they usually possess the ability to be wise and philosophical in their understanding of personal freedom. The wings of Jupiter indicate the potential the planet gives for swift, poised, spiritual flight—or for sinking deep into earthly bondage like Icarus, whose wings of wax (still of materiality and not forged from the spirit) melted under the truth testing of the sun.

In mythology, Jupiter was the ruling Olympian deity, guardian of the law, upholder of justice and virtue, and champion of the truth. His father was Chronos who feared displacement by his children and so ate them at birth. Jupiter was saved by his mother, Rhea, who offered Chronos a stone in Jupiter's stead. Jupiter himself sired four children: Mercury, Diana (moon), Apollo (god of the sun and prophesy), and Dionysus (god of wine). Jupiter wielded the thunderbolt, and the oak, the mountain summit, and the eagle were sacred to him. His crown was a wreath of oak leaves, and he was often identified with the Oak-Man or Old Man Oak (as was Robin Hood, associated with Jupiter and his son Mercury). His voice was said to be heard in the rustle of oak leaves. He held a scepter, a thunderbolt, and a figure of victory.

Zodiac

SAGITTARIUS—ARCHER
NOVEMBER 22–DECEMBER 21

ANGEL: Sachiel
RULING PLANET: Jupiter

KEYWORD: Wisdom

AGE: 35-42 (attainment of maturity)

METAL: Tin

CROSS: Mutable

ELEMENT: Fire

QUALITIES: Honesty, clarity, dignity, benevolence, magnanimity, jollity, encompassing quality, optimism, loyalty, independence, generosity, love of education, literature, justice

ILLNESSES TO GUARD AGAINST: Rheumatism or arthritis in the hips, thighs, and lower limbs; sciatica, sprains, hip dislocation, fracture of the thighs; nervous disorders, lung and throat afflictions, bronchitis, high blood pressure

BODY AREAS: Hips, thighs, arteries

STONES: Sapphire, amethyst, topaz, diamond

NUMBERS: 3, 4

DAY: Thursday

FLOWERS AND HERBS: Carnation, wallflower, clove-pink, sage

TREE: Mulberry, vine, chestnut

ANIMALS: Mare, lion, unicorn

BIRDS: Eagle, peacock, bird of paradise

COLORS: Lilac, mauve, purple, amethyst, violet, indigo, vermilion, midnight blue.

The name *Sagittarius* is derived from the early (*Semivir* ("half-man") and from the Roman *Saggitifer* ("arrow-carrier").

editation on Jupiter

Light a yellow candle at Sachiel's hour (midnight, 8 A.M., or 4 P.M.) and think of the huge radiant presence of Jupiter as he treads the firmament in rhythmic, regular mode—beneficent, humorous, and generous.

> Lord Jupiter, I contemplate your qualities of magnanimity, mercy, and charity, essential components of justice and wisdom, as I study this candle flame. I ask

to be endowed with your gifts of expansive vision, love of freedom, and wide-ranging philosophy. I meditate upon your jovial nature, your generosity and abundance, your kindly candid quality, which brings astuteness and discernment to all matters of judgement.

I concentrate on absorbing your virtues of confidence, good humor and tolerance, and pray to be endued with these qualities in harmony and balance, so that they accord with the true needs of my nature.

Repeat the meditation three times, then sit and allow the benefits you have asked for to wash through your mind as you watch the candle burn down.

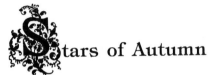tars of Autumn

Pisces, the Fishes, has no bright stars, but its two main streams are symmetrically arranged, beginning at the borders of Aquarius. To the left of Aquarius and lying lower in the heavens is Cetus, the Whale. The shape of this spacious constellation has been compared to a lounge chair. One of the stars that mark its headrest is Mira Ceti ("the wonderful star of Cetus"), a variable star that exhibits strange behavior. Sometimes its light swells to the first magnitude while, at other times, it varies between the third to the ninth magnitude.

Higher than Cetus, to the left of Pisces and the right of Taurus, shines Aries, the Ram. It has only four bright stars and has been displaced by Pisces as the vernal equinox, due to pole precession.

Above Aquarius, in a dark part of the sky, strides Pegasus, or the Winged Horse. It is easy to recognize the Great Square of Pegasus, which is huge and richly illuminated by a jewellike setting of brilliant stars against almost black velvet, for few stars are visible within the square itself.

One of the four stars of the Square actually belongs to Andromeda, next to Pegasus. Andromeda's name designates her as "the Chained Woman." The Great Nebula in Andromeda can be seen with the unaided eye, visible as a faint pearly luster. We now know that it is not nebula (cosmic dust irradiated by nearby stars) but is actually another galaxy or stellar system, coequal with our own, shining 680,000 light-years away in outer space; it is our nearest galaxy.

Between Andromeda and Aries shines the little constellation of Triangulum, the Triangle. This group is thought by some to represent the Ass (the triangle forming the shape of its ears). The Ass represents the dark side of Aries, suggesting the spiritual state of ignorance and benightedness that may befall humanity if the Aries lessons are not heeded. As the gods and sacred animals of old are represented in the heavens, so it is believed that this shadowy little constellation might also be the sigil for a sinister and secret ass cult said to have been practiced in Jerusalem and initiated in the age of Aries.

ISEWOMAN'S JOURNAL

Dreaming Bannocks

On the twenty-ninth day of November, which is St Andrew's Eve, it is a treat to make "dreaming bannocks." The recipe is Scottish, and the bannocks are very good.

Take a generous portion of eggs and flour and best butter, enough to bake cakes for all the company, mix well together and put in plenty of salt and a dash of cinnamon. Then, for each separate cake that the mixture makes, you must add a tiny pinch of soot, hardly bigger than a pinhead. Bless the cakes as you form them out of the dough, and toast them well on the gridiron; but this must be done silently, for it is said the baker must be as mute as a stone while baking and toasting, for one word would destroy the whole concern.

Give one or more of the cakes to those who are trying the spell with you, and save a couple for your own supper morsel.

Then must you all retire to bed in perfect silence, where you will be sure to fall into slumber and see wonderful emblems of your destiny. To some, their sweethearts appear in spirit guise and give forth solemn pronouncements concerning their future life and its fated pathways.

Author's Note

St. Andrew, Scotland's patron saint, was both saint and apostle. He was a fisherman in Bethsaida, a follower of John the Baptist, who afterward joined Jesus Christ. He and his brother Simon Peter were the first to be called to apostleship so that they might become "fishers of men." He attended the feeding of the five thousand and was among those who, on the Mount of Olives, heard the prophecy of the fall of Jerusalem. He is reputed to have preached in Scythia. He was martyred at Patras in A.D. 70, bound to a cross decussate (X). His relics were said to have been removed to Constantinople (now Istanbul), some of them being transported to Scotland in the eighth century. *Andrew* is Greek for "a man," especially one of simple, powerful, magnetic, and spiritual qualities that are applicable to the character of the saint. They are also virtues generally beloved and esteemed by the Scots; this might be part of the reason he was chosen as patron saint for ancient Caledonia.

Charm to Make Your Pennies Grow

Upon the night of the first new moon, which is Bride's moon, you must hold out in the palm of your left hand a shiny silver coin, as new as may be. Say to the crescent moon:

Moon penny bright as silver
Come and play with little childer.

Imagine a shower of such coins falling into your upturned palms; pass the coin you hold from your left hand to your right. Then make good and sure that, when your ship of fortune docks, others share its cargo with you, a tenth part at least, or you will fare worse than when you started. When you work charms for money-luck, it is good to carry the satin pod of the herb honesty from one moon to the next. The "silver pieces" of honesty are beloved of the moonlight fairies, who will bless your endeavors.

Left Shoe and New Moon Charm

On the night of the new moon, you must take a pair of shoes you have been wearing all week, drop a new penny into the left shoe, and, going to your chamber window, hold it up to the moon and speak these words through the open casement:

> Luna, be my friend tonight;
> Let my fortune take its flight,
> May my shoe a Moon-boat be
> Silver and gold sail back to me.

Then put your two shoes together underneath your bed, and do not disturb them or take the penny out until the moon waxes to full. Afterward, you must give some of your newfound wealth to the angels, or it will vanish away.

Author's Note

These two charms and chants for wealth, or "pennies," were generally used by children, as is indicated by their wording and imagery. As sublunary creatures, however, we are all children of the moon goddess. There is no reason, therefore, that these charms should not prove just as efficacious for adults. To "give some of your newfound wealth to the angels" means that a portion of any increase in income over the allotted two-week period of the moon's "waxing to full" must be given freely to those in need. It is part of arcane lore that if this tradition is not honored, the angels who have humanity in their care will so direct the outcome of events that money acquired by occult means, however simple they may be, will disappear through accidental and unforeseen expenditure, therefore conferring no benefit on the recipient.

Spell to Charm Away the Hiccoughs

Take a few dill seeds and chew them well with a long draught of water. Hold your breath and say this rune three times over:

> Hiccough Sprite, it's time you flew,
> Today's your day to bake and brew.

ISEWOMAN'S WEATHERBOOK

When storms rage, folk say that Thor the Thunder God is hammering in his forge; so you must be careful to put away all metal objects, for fear they attract his attention and his power strikes them; but the powers of the goddess are alive, too, in the thunder and lightning of the storm, and so it is well to cover your mirrors, for it is the magic in these that attracts her; and if the lightning spirit gets into your house, be sure to open the doors and windows wide to let her escape, or she will do more damage than a trapped bull. Carry a bay leaf or a sprig of dried may blossom (plucked at night, when it is fragrant with its occult perfume) about your person to protect you from being struck by lightning, and never shelter beneath a tree, even Old Man Oak, for he cannot always refuse the withering kiss of the lightning.

❧

If you see a rainbow in the morning, pelting rain will not be long in coming; but the sun will be behind it to make the sky like a pewter dish, and the rain will fall and fall prettily like showers of silver elf-bolts.

❧

If you see a rainbow in the evening, it is as fair a token of the sun on the morrow as is a sky of crimson, the "shepherd's delight."

❧

When you see glimpses of a rainbow all broken up by a cloudy sky, and those clouds sailing fast like ships at full mast, the wind that drives them will rise and increase, storms will come and even afterward the wind will remain all of a bluster-and-a-fluster; that is why those gleams and glimpses of parts of the rainbow are called wind-dogs; and if you whistle to them, you'll change the direction of the wind.

❧

If there's enough bright blue sky to cut cloth for making a sailor a pair of trousers, the day'll turn out fine, no matter how rain and squalls threaten; but if the sky be a pale, wish-washed blue between the clouds, then no matter if you could sew trousers for the whole crew, the rain and the squalls will have the lion's share of the day.

❧

When you mend your fire, go outdoors and study the smoke as it issues from the chimney pot; if it makes a rising fountain into the heavens, then it is keeping its secrets and will tell you nothing; but if it falls like the specter of a serpent and disperses lower than the rooftop, rainy weather may be expected.

❧

When the sun's noonday rays are bright and glittering as crystals and diamonds, sparkling with more than their custom-ary brilliance, rainy weather will soon be upon us.

When the doves around a dovecote are busy and restless, fluttering back home and then taking flight again, as if they know not where they want to be, and a note comes into their gentle songs that is keen and haunting, they are letting you know that a change of weather is already in the air.

When the sun rises like a lump of metal fervent-heated in the blacksmith's forge, golden and heavy and solid as if it were a sovereign and without rays or a halo, then expect grand weather, full of glory.

Look for a ring around the sun as it sets, which will be flaming and brilliant like a golden ruby and seeming to light up a magical world behind the clouds; when you see that halo, you can be sure of brightness and beauty for next day's weather.

Chapter Ten

DECEMBER

Yuletide: The Hawk of Winter

Old Man Winter

Old Man Winter walks with snow-shod feet
Hangs hoar on the briar and whistles through the sleet;
Crackling ice without makes home-fire sing
Old Man Winter, Christmas he doth bring;
Early draws away the day
With fingers of frozen clay.
His glance the tender garden mars
His breath makes brilliant the stars.

Sarah Greaves

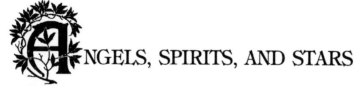

ANGELS, SPIRITS, AND STARS

Capricorn is represented as a goat-fish, a strange horned animal with a dolphin's tail, its right foot raised as though it is tripping lightly, gazellelike. There is a link between Capricorn and Sagittarius, a mirror reflection in their mutations. Capricorn himself was once called "the centaur archer," because the beginning of the winter solstice anciently occurred on the sun's entry into Capricorn; since those times the stars have advanced to the east, and now the solstice begins at the sun's entry into Sagittarius. The Archer's sigil shows a human head and torso emerging from a perfected animal body, while that for Capricorn depicts an animal head and forelegs emerging from a fish, implying that Capricorn is mysteriously linked with our deepest origins in the great causal ocean of life, the watery womb of the Mother from which everything on earth, and the earth herself, has come forth.

Bearing this in mind, it is interesting that Capricorn is the sign that ushers in Christmas, the birth of the Child of Light from Divine Mother, symbolized by the sun seeming to turn in his course after the longest earthly night on December 24, so that life and light begin to make a triumphant return. Perhaps in its deeper symbolism, Capricorn signifies Christ in nature, for the sign of the Christ is the fish. The mystic principle of the spiritual light aglow in every manifestation of the natural world is one that has been deeply rejected by Christian orthodoxy in the past; this rejection has led, inevitably, to the violation of the planet and the identification of Pan, god of nature and of earth, with the "devil." And yet all the while the Great God Pan has been up there in the stars, bringing in Christmas and bound heart and soul to the Christ. As we rediscover this indwelling principle, which animates nature in all her beauty and myriad forms, we shall once again, as in the far distant past, become attuned to our planet and the universe. It is said that angels shall once more "walk with men."

In mundane astrology, Capricorn is the mountain goat always striving for the summits. He rules the tenth house of careers, professions, and worldly status. He lends qualities of resolution, determination, and independence. Capricorn people tend to be hardworking, self-sacrificing, cautious, reliable, systematic, ambitious, honest, and aloof. They are natural disciplinarians and often assume power and responsibility. Capricornians wish to discipline the vigor of the life forces leaping deep within themselves; sometimes they can be unwise in their application of discipline and repress and deny rather than control and modulate.

Saturn, ruler of Capricorn, is a spiritual influence which gives peace, serenity, and a rich harvest in later life; so, in their mature years, usually tranquil after toiling ambitiously up the mountainside, Capricornians can turn to the waters of the soul once again, entering on some form of spiritual service to life as they seek inner wisdom and enlightenment. This embracing of the "waters" (an eternal symbol for the deeper self) late in life must be undertaken so that they may attain to the stars, or the heights of human consciousness. Such seems to be the spiritual truth in the story of Pan (god of the vital life forces in nature and the earth) flinging himself into the "waters" so that he might be lifted by God (Jupiter) up to the "stars." Capricornians need to achieve at an earthly level, shepherding the strong forces of life within them (Pan is also the god of shepherds), so that they might move toward applying the lessons of dogged effort and indefatigable determination, learned so thoroughly in material terms, to the dimensions of spirit and spiritual service. For Capricornians, both the mountain summit and the waters represent the heights to which they aspire.

In mythology, Saturn is Chronos, the god of time. His ponderous, measured movement identified him with stately old age. He is the spirit of age, rigidity, gravity, restriction, control; he also personifies understanding, experience, and kindly restraint. He withholds until the time is right. His scythe reaps the golden treasure of the corn, the harvest of human life, so that it may be ground into the divine bread; when he destroys, he is fearful, but his destructiveness is never wanton. He clears away outmoded and unwanted conditions; he breaks the mold so that new inspiration may be born. He is concentric and steady, the spirit of constancy and long sight. He teaches forbearance in suffering, the worth of travail and adherence to the grindstone, love of tradition as a framework of reference for eternal truth, respect for the law and constancy in human relationships. He is the Reflective Intellect, the Stilled Soul, the Watcher on the Threshold. His chariot is drawn by dragons and griffins (both of them fabulous creatures of the psyche or mind), which guard hidden treasure (the dragon is the great symbol of the rampant undifferentiated forces upon which Capricorn focuses).

Saturnus was the god of agriculture (note his association with Pan) and the instigator of civilization and social order. He overthrew his father, Uranus, the first ruling godhead, arming himself with a flint and a sickle (tools for burning and reaping, the flint stressing Saturn's supremacy over matter in its heaviest and most solidifed form—rock, crystal, and precious stones, and also the skeletal structure of animal and human bodies). Uranus cursed him, predicting that he would suffer the same fate; and so it was that Jupiter, god of freedom, banished him to outer space. Jupiter was Saturn's own son, saved at birth from being devoured by his father, the fate suffered by Saturn's other children.

Spiritual truth seems here to imply that Saturn is the god of the space-matter-time continuum, which creates a universe that is constantly recycling itself by courtesy of the agency of time. All that is born of earth must die, in time, and return to clay; yet when the consciousness of humanity has attained to true freedom, time itself may be transcended and overcome.

 odiac

CAPRICORN—GOAT-FISH
DECEMBER 22–JANUARY 19

ANGEL: Cassiel

RULING PLANET: Saturn

KEYWORD: Achievement

AGE: 42–49 (early middle age and, with Pluto, old age)

METAL: Lead

CROSS: Cardinal

ELEMENT: Earth

QUALITIES: Responsibility, duty, toil, enquiry, restraint, secrecy, discipline, patience, persistence, doggedness, indefatigable aspiration, limitation, taciturnity, practicality, idealism, melancholia, imprisonment

ILLNESSES TO GUARD AGAINST: Childhood ills, illness and injury that affects the knees, skin diseases, chills, arthritis, toothache, earache, migraine and headache, depression, anxiety neurosis, mood swings

BODY AREA: Knees

STONES: Onyx, obsidian, jet, garnet, jade, opal, ruby (dark), sapphire, zircon

NUMBERS: 3, 8

DAY: Saturday

FLOWERS AND HERBS: Nightshade, rue, snowdrop, Solomon's seal

TREES: Pine, cypress, yew, spruce, holly

ANIMALS: Dog, elephant, goat, bear

BIRDS: Owl, falcon

COLORS: Black, gray, violet, dark brown, dun, shades of earth

Capricorn relates to the god of nature, Pan, who flung himself into the Nile to escape from the great god Typhon, becoming "crowned with horns" (Capricornus) as part goat, part fish; at this transformation, Jupiter lifted him into the skies to become one of the zodiacal constellations.

editation on Saturn

Light an autumn-brown candle at Cassiel's hour (3 A.M., 11 A.M. or 7 P.M.) and begin to think of the great planet Saturn as it turns in space.

> Lord Saturn, I see your marvelous globe with the eye of my inner vision; its color glows a mysterious and holy blue, encircled with its strange ring-systems, three in number, each radiantly golden. Your spirit descending from this lovely sphere brings me the power to govern myself wisely, patience and perseverance to accomplish, the millstone grit to try again despite setbacks and disappointment. You give me the ability calmly to reflect upon my individuality so that I may seek to correct my personal weaknesses. I call upon your strength to guide me in times of abundance and adversity, and I give thanks for the gift of your bitter fruits of justice whose nourishment I need.

tars of Winter

Look for Orion in the winter months, the most majestic of the constellations. It rises toward the east, sails in brilliant splendor between the horizon and the zenith, and sets almost due west. Its four bright stars form a quadrilateral, in the midst of which are three stars nearly as radiant, slanting downward. Its brightest star, at the top left-hand corner of the quadrilateral, is Alpha Orionis or Betelgeux (Giant's

Shoulder), which glows with red ember light. Rigel, the star in the lower right-hand corner, glitters with a blue-white radiance and is more vivid than Betelgeuse; it is Orion's second star and was once less powerful than the Giant's Shoulder. Its name means Giant's Leg. In the top right-hand corner is the star Bellatrix (Female Warrior). The quadrilateral's southeast corner is formed by Kappa, a second-magnitude star. The Great Nebula in Orion is famous, and is located in the Sword of Orion—represented by a line of three stars; it is a cloud-bed of shining cosmic dust, illumined by the radiance of the stars that cluster in it, at rest deep in outer space.

The Giant's Shoulder forms a beautifully luminous equilateral triangle with Sirius in the Great Dog (Canis Procyon Major) and in the Little Dog (Canis Minor). This Great Triangle is one of the most vivid constellations of the heavens. Procyon is golden, while Sirius glitters with a snow-and-sea blue-white radiance. Sirius, the Dog Star, is the most powerful in the star group of Canis Major, as beautiful and brilliant as our own rising sun when viewed through a telescope. The intensity of its light is due to the fact that it is a near star.

Orion was a giant hunter, noble and beautiful in form and face. He was blinded by an enemy (Enopion), but the god Vulcan sent Cedalion to be his guide, and his eyes were healed by turning them to the sun. Diana, female warrior and huntress, put him to death, whereupon he was transfigured into one of the constellations. He is supposed to be attended by stormy weather, representative of the passions that played about his mortal life. Every hunter has a horse and a dog; the dogs that accompany Orion are well-known features of the heavens; less well known is the Horsehead nebula in Orion, which literally resembles a horse's head.

The Circumpolar Stars

The circumpolar stars are those that, in the northern heavens, are so close to the Pole that they do not rise above the horizon or set to sink below it, but travel around it in unceasing circles. They are visible every night of the year, if the skies are clear, although their positions differ with the seasons. The most obvious circumpolar configuration in the sky is the famous Ursa Major, also called the Plow, the Great Bear, Charles's Wain, and the Big Dipper.

These seven stars are most easily identified in the autumn, and form an irregular square, the Plow handle extending upward in a gentle curve from the star at the top left-hand corner of the quadrilateral (the smallest star of the four, forming part of the "handle"). The seven stars all have Arabic names and, working from the top right-hand corner, down, across, up, and then along the handle are: Dubhe (bear), Merak (loin of the bear), Phecda (bear's thigh), Megrez (root of bear's tail), Alioth (fat tail of a sheep), Mizar which doubles with Alcor (rider), and, finally, Alkaid or Benetnasch (chief of the mourners). Within the Great Bear is the famous planetary owl nebula, shaped like a staring owl.

WISEWOMAN'S JOURNAL

Fairy Oil

This oil is to be made up in spring and left to settle so that it can be put to use on the Fairy Days. Christmas is a time when we may contemplate all the four elements at peace in Christ; and so herbs, minerals, animals, human beings, fairies, and angels, all the kingdoms and queendoms of the godhead, have their ambassador in the Christmas Story. The patient animals, the stone floor of the Christmas cave, the wooden manger filled with sweet fragrant hay, the angels and fairies of earth, air, fire, and water, all were there. We may like to think of a little fire burning in a pot in the Christmas cave to give warmth, and water nearby for refreshment. Outside, the Star gives forth its pure radiance to heaven and earth, and the Angels sing. Fate decreed that Mary and Joseph could not reside in the Inn, for that was the World, and its doors cut off men and women from their true heritage and lock them up inside their own self-consciousness, which is Isolation.

So the Christ was born in humanity's true home, which is not the World, but the cave of the Heart, which is God's Heart, where all live in harmony, joy, and love. This is why it is said that the fairies may be seen at Christmastime, and an old spell there is that gives directions for making a Fairy Oil that will enable one to look into the magical fairy worlds.

Sweet herbs and summer flowers have many potencies, and it is good to use these; but they cannot do all the work for you. You must prepare your own soul so that you may see fairies; and this means loving them and their world of nature, loving the Great Heart that holds us all, and seeking them in their haunts at the right time and in the right way. Thus may you see the fairies, and if you prepare the oil, prepare it with a charm of your own at the hours of Sachiel (1 A.M., 8 A.M., OR 3 P.M.), and let your charm be a prayer to the god of meadows and forests, and the Great God and Goddess of All, that you may enter the fairy realm without harm, that the fairies may come to know and love you, and that you may know and love them.

Here is the wort-cunning* to be followed in preparing the Fairy Oil: put a tankard of corn oil into a green glass jar and bless it with charms. Gather eglantine, the leaves of the briar, the buds of the hollyhock, the flowers of wild thyme (the young ripening tops of the fragrant wild grass), the shooting buds of young hazel, yarrow flowers and rue, and the sweet grass from inside a fairy ring. Pluck some marigold flowers from the garden. If you do not have any, the field marigold will suffice. Gather your herbs and flowers from those that grow toward the east, and at Cassiel's hour, steep your posy in the corn oil. Leave it to ripen in the sun (the jar must be covered or stoppered) for

* *Wort-cunning* means herb-cunning—a knowledge of herbal lore and medicine handed down from generation to generation by the herbhealers.

three days; then you may pour out the oil into smaller glass jars, as small as may be. Into each one put seven drops of rose oil, and stopper well. A light touch of the oil is to be put on to your eyelids, upon your brow, into the hollow of the throat, on to each fingertip and rubbed into the wrists before proceeding into the wild. It would be well to do this at Cassiel's hour or Sachiel's hour, if you conveniently may; and then you must venture out alone to see the fairies, even if that be only into your own garden under the early moon, or just at sunrise, noon, or as the evening dew falls. If you can wash your eyes in the pure dew, which some say is the sweat of the stars, that is good; and mark well the Fairy Days, though others may be tried, for the fairies are always with us.

The Wishing Box

Now here is a way to make for loved ones a magical gift that they will always treasure.

Take a box of scented wood, exquisitely carved; and if you cannot procure scented wood, then line it with velvet and fine pure silk, and in the lining conceal the dried leaves of lavender and thyme and freshly plucked rosemary. Here is how the spell is to be essayed: polish the wood tenderly and with industry until the highlighted grain appears in all its beauty. Place in the basket three rose leaves, or, if they be withered on the stem, three leaves of the bay. Go out into the evening of the first full moon of the year, when she is well risen and riding the skies, and the stars are as sharp and bright as vixen's eyes. Hold the box open to the heavens and say:

> Oh Gracious Queen, Lady fair
> May Moon and stars heed my prayer;

Upon this box let blessings fall
For my true love* its gifts enthrall.

You must work this magic for three nights running before midnight each time, and then thereafter will the box be charmed.

Now you must write a spell on virgin paper and, having sealed it with wax from a thrice-burnt candle, place it inside the casket.

This is how your spell should read: Take three slips of paper, no bigger than elf-bolts; inscribe upon them in a tiny hand as if it were writ by fairies, the three wishes of your heart's desire. Fold each around a rose leaf (or the leaf of the bay tree) and place diligently and respectfully within the silken interior of the box. Shut up the lid and leave the box alone until the wishes are granted. Then may you write new ones, always three at a time.

If you cannot contrive to line your friend's or your love's Wishing Box with silk or velvet, but must leave it bare inside, then be very sure to place within a linen handkerchief, all clean and new and a pure snowy white, and have your friend or your lover wrap their wishbound leaves in that.

Charm to Soothe an Ailing Child

Hush Poppet, sleep tight!
And Little Nanny Buttoncap
Will come to you tonight.

She'll bring you three wishes
From the King of all the Fishes
And one from Mother Mary
And one from the Queen of Fairies.

And when you awake
At tomorrow's morn
You'll see three Golden Birds

* If the box is to be a gift for someone other than your true love, then insert his or her name accordingly.

As the new day is born
And blessed you'll be
With three Golden Words
And the Sun will smile on you
And on Land and on sea
And blessed you'll be.

So hush Poppet, sleep tight!
And Little Nanny Buttoncap
Will come to you tonight.

The Charm has a circular motion in the saying so that it may be repeated or sung over and over again until the child falls asleep.

Daemon Fire

First, find a receptacle of good strong metal; silver is best. Take it out under the full moon, which is the night of the goddess. Wash the silver basin under the risen moon's rays, turning it this way and that.

Have handfuls of pine cones ready. Place the basin on stone, making sure all is safe and well, and light the cones with the wick of a white candle. The basin should be deep, so that you do yourself no harm.

Sprinkle dried sprigs of lavender upon the little leaping flames, and let the cones burn until they turn red.

Put no more now upon your Daemon Fire, but gaze into its embers.

In this magical fire you will see ghosts of the past and dreams of the future. You will see fairy birds and strange mythical beasts. And if luck is with you, when the fire has died quite away until there is nothing more than a trailing phantom of pine and lavender incense and a whisper of falling ashes, you may go outside to the woods and the fields and the lonely places and follow the moonbeams to find the fairy haunts.

WISEWOMAN'S WEATHERBOOK

When the moon wears a rusty bonnet, there'll be rain clouds and fickle weather.

≫

When the sky grows gray and heavy in the wintertime, and there's a sparkle behind it like shooting stars, snow will soon start to fall like great soft goosefeathers; if the wind begins to softly moan and softly whittle, then the snowstorm will go round and round the house like a fine lady, and leave a white glove in every window.

≫

When a rooster crows in the rain, he's crying, "Sunshine— soon! Sunshine—soon!" and you can be sure dry and droughty weather is on its way.

≫

As the high summer passes away, the Angel of the Year folds her wings and summons the sacred fire from the deeps of the earth before she falls into stillness and sleep; watch for this fire as it sets the trees and the grasses aflame and celebrates the last of the gathering-in and the harvest, stores for the coming winter; and if this fire (which is all the autumn colors) touches the trees early, and the migratory birds flock together and teem and whirl in the sky before the last of the late summer is gone, then expect a stubborn and nagging winter with a scattering of hard frosts and clammy fogs that make the bushes weep, one that ushers in a feeble and sickly spring that can't struggle up on to its pins and get going until the latter end of May.

≫

When in autumn and wintertime the sinking sun is like a ruby in a betrothal ring, expect galloping winds from the north and northwest; and when in those seasons the sun at its rising is the color of a deep-hued wine, you may expect similar ruffianly winds to come blustering from the south and southeast.

When your dog barks and frolics and chases his tail, when he jumps at a shadow and will not be still, he is anticipating a change of weather.

Be wary of pointing at a rainbow, for you'll make the rain come back; and honor the rainbow spirit, because then he'll be likely to guide your soul across his bridge into the secret worlds when you fall asleep and dream at night.

When the Northern Lights dance in the firmament, there's a storm brewing as boisterous as a gang of bairns; and if you search for them by starlight, you'll see the fairies.

When in the wintertime the stars shine bright as new buttons, it'll be champion weather next day; but if they're dim and fogged over and flicker like jack-o'-lanterns, you can be sure of rain and restlessness.

If in the autumn or the wintertime, or yet the early spring, you should see the beasts of the fields, the horses and the cattle, standing together in little bands and breathing the breath one of another, then you will know it's bound to be a cold day and hoary, and you can expect no better for a short while at least.

When you stand at your bedchamber window in the wintertime and look out upon the firmament, or yet take a walk by starlight in the warm evenings of the year and behold the sky alive with strange flashes and globes of fire and stars falling and traveling like will-o'-the-wisps across the heavens, the weather will wax boisterous and temperamental until the next quarter moon.

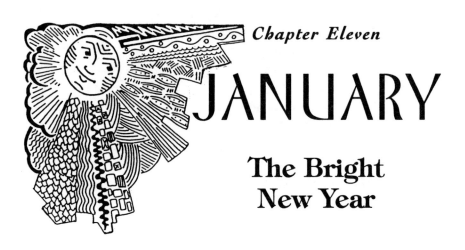

Chapter Eleven

JANUARY

The Bright
New Year

The January Man

Oh the January Man
He walks the road in woollen coat
And boots of leather.

The February Man still shakes the snow
From off his hair and blows his hands.

The Man of March he sees the spring
And wonders what the year will bring
And hopes for better weather.

And through the April rain the Man
Goes down to watch the birds come in
To share the summer.

The Man of May stands very still
Watching the children dance away the day.

In June the man inside the Man
Is young and wants to lend a hand
And grins at each new color.

And in July the Man
In cotton shirt he sits and thinks on being idle.

The August Man in thousands takes the road
To watch the sea and find the sun.

September Man is standing near
To saddle up and leave the year
And Autumn is his bridle.

And the Man of new October
Takes the reins and early frost
Is on his shoulders.

The poor November Man sees fire and rain
And snow and mist and winter gale.

December Man looks through the snow
To let eleven brothers know they're all a little older.

And the January Man
Comes round again in woollen clothes
And boots of leather
To take another turn and walk along
The icy road he knows so well.

Oh the January Man is here, for starting each
 and every year
Along the road forever . . .

David Goulder

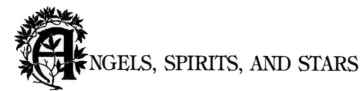

NGELS, SPIRITS, AND STARS

With the coming of the Age of Aquarius,* that golden age of marvels upon whose threshold we stand, our old and outworn concepts begin to dissolve away, their shackles loosed by the two-thousand-year lesson of the Piscean Age, which is drawing to a close. The ideal of the Good Shepherd, as it applies to worldly affairs, is seen to be outmoded. Relying on personal figures who assume leadership or upon the prescribed mores and morals of the establishment no longer seems invariably wise. There have been, and continue to be, too many brutal regimes, too many police states, too many dictatorships. We begin to perceive that those structures that were once thought to be the very

* The official date for the Age of Aquarius is the year 2010.

bedrock of civilization were possibly only ever meant to be temporary, a composite cradle in which we whiled away our earliest infancy, no longer appropriate as the day begins to dawn that we will not have to spend largely in sleeping. The vision of true, awakened consciousnes begins to grasp us.

Aquarius, the water-bearer, holds forth his pitcher of water; already the first few drops of the deluge have reached those who can recognize their own thirst. There will be a second Flood, but not in any negative or destructive sense. That necessary lesson has been undergone, its historical baptism of the world has passed into myth; the water initiation is a thing of the past, its teachings part of the stronghold of the communal human soul.

The waters that will cause the deluge this time are none other than the waters of consciousness itself. The Aquarius constellation, as divinely imagined by the ancients, shows that there are fish in the stream of water descending earthward from the heavenly pitcher; fish that symbolize Christ, the Light of the World. Yet these fish are reborn because the sacrifice of the Piscean avatar, demonstrated by the crucifixion as the great sacrifice each individual soul must make in reaching for enlightenment, has achieved its great aim. The umbilical cord that binds and constrains the Two Fishes of the Pisces sigil (always representing the fishes as bound to one another) is broken at last. Jupiter's dream of freedom for the Neptunian fish-souls is, in the fullness of time, joyfully realized. The brotherhood of man is no longer a restraining shackle, because men and women are no longer fettered by the chains of their own selfish egotistical striving. The element in which the reborn fishes live and move and have their being is none other than the divine airs of the godhead itself, and this very freedom is the source of their brotherhood. Aquarius as the airy sign pours forth the waters, which are the airs of the new age, and it is our consciousness, the mind in the heart, that is deluged, not the body of Mother Earth.

Two planets rule Aquarius. Saturn, the stern restrainer and disciplinarian who is exalted in Libra (the Scales) and who tests our patience and endurance with his severities, co-rules the sign with that fascinating planet, Uranus, whom occultists and seers hail as the great influence for the new age. The thought of Uranus immediately brings electricity to mind, the stuff of subtle intense power, brightness, and invisibility, surely the stolen god-fire of Prometheus, magical, supernatural, and instinctive with celerity and the blue sparks of crackling life. However true these associations might be, Uranus, like Saturn, is an imprisoner. He cast his children into Tartarus, or Hades, so that they were sealed in the womb of Gaia, locked into the body of Mother Earth. But, of course, this is necessary to the process of birth. The child who falls out of the womb before the time is right (Saturn, or Chronos, god of time, sets his pendulum in motion so that his calculations are exact) cannot live, cannot even be created. If rushing, hurrying humanity had its way, the plan of creation would be aborted.

Mythology tells us that Uranus was the first god—the beloved son of Gaia who sprang from the original Source (empty space), known as Chaos. He was therefore the first-born son of the Mother; this links him with the esoteric Christ, or the Third Principle, the Son of Light. His further link with the Christ forces exists in his association with electricity. Uranus is the planet of the mind (the sign he rules, Aquarius, is an air sign, and air relates to the mind). It is associated with sudden and devastating upheavals and unexpected change. It is the enemy of premeditation. Like Neptune and Pluto, the influence of Uranus is to be seen in trends and historical events rather than in the narrow sphere of the individual. It rules the genius that reaches past the limitations of the intellect. It is the lord of revolutions, and the breathtaking Bolshevik revolution; its equally sudden and unexpected dissolution exhibit typical Uranian-inspired qualities. It is the planet of intuition, of warning dreams and second sight, of electricity, magnetism, waking visions, inventions, life-changing scientific discoveries, astrology, and astronomy—Urania, the feminine aspect of the great spiritual being that we call Uranus, is the muse of astronomy. Uranus disrupts, shocks, separates, rebels, electrifies, explodes, and reforms. It demolishes in order to rebuild. When its influences are negatively received, it can inspire sexual perversion and anarchy.

Being bombarded by its vibrations, it is just as well that Aquarians also receive the restraining and constricting influence of Saturn. Uranus can cause shattering and sudden nervous breakdowns, but Saturn's steadying influence shelters those born under Aquarius. These people are far-seeing, ahead of their time, eccentric (apparently), humanitarian, and altruistic. They are interested in groups, in fellowship, friendship, and interpersonal relationships. They are interested in the individual within the context of a functioning group. They are more fascinated by group dynamics—how people respond and react to the sparks created by one another—than by personalities. They are influenced (and sometimes dogged) by unexpected happenings. They need to use and expand their minds and to assert control, creatively and correctly applied, at all levels of mental functioning, from the highest to the lowest. Their great life themes are communication and relationship. Their sense of brotherhood stems from this, for we all breathe the same air*—even the fishes of Pisces need oxygen. Thought control will be the challenge of the new age and is the lesson of Aquarius. Communication and relationship between the heart-mind and the frontal mind is the essential challenge by which we may usher in the Age of Aquarius.

odiac

AQUARIUS—WATER-BEARER
JANUARY 20–FEBRUARY 18

ANGELS: Uriel or Auriel, Cassiel

RULING PLANETS: Saturn and Uranus

KEYWORD: Brotherhood

AGE: 49–56 (middle age—a second flowering)

METAL: Uranium

CROSS: Fixed

ELEMENT: Air

QUALITIES: Independence, turbulence, fellowship, friendship, relationship, originality, genius, brotherhood, abstraction, optimism, intellect, remoteness, literature, science, inventiveness, peace, artistry, inspiration, perversity, tenacity, intuition, depression

ILLNESSES TO GUARD AGAINST: Weakness and injury affecting the ankles, depression, anxiety, hysteria, nervous breakdowns, spasms, fits, paralysis, convulsive disorders, broken bones, poor circulation, varicose veins, rheumatism, electric shocks, danger from lightning

---

* As Chief Seattle pointed out so astutely in his famous statement.

BODY AREAS: Circulatory system, nervous system, ankles, shins, bones

STONES: Zircon, amber, amethyst, garnet, malachite, ruby, jet, black onyx, jacinth, jargon, jade, opal, ruby

NUMBERS: 2, 3

DAY: Saturday

FLOWERS AND HERBS: Snowdrop, foxglove, mullein (torchflower), gentian, great valerian

TREES: Pine

ANIMALS: Dog, otter

BIRDS: Cuckoo, albatross, phoenix

COLORS: All colors of the spectrum, particularly electric and ultramarine blue, electric green, deep violet

The Aquarian constellation was anciently called *Shabatu* ("curse of rain") and formed the eleventh book of the Babylonian *Epic of Creation* (Aquarius is the eleventh zodiacal sign). The time when the sun is in Aquarius corresponds to the time when the waters of the Nile are still high.

editation on Uranus

Light a gold or yellow candle, and dedicate it to Uriel, the archangel of Uranus, at 2 A.M., 10 A.M. or 6 P.M.

> Lord Uranus, Lady Urania, let me be filled harmoniously with your liberating spirit. Let me see the long view, the greater vision, which is yours. Teach me to see which conditions and circumstances in my outer life I must let go so that I can avoid clinging to outmoded structures. Teach me to use your revolutionary forces constructively and lovingly so that they lead to true evolution. Help me to ride your incoming tides so that I might partake of your higher spheres in which are the gifts of vision and prophecy. I ask that I may absorb and harmonize your energies so that spiritual electricity constantly revitalizes and elevates my mental bodies.

Visualize the power of Uranus streaming down through your mind-centers as you watch the candle burn down.

Stars of Winter

Above Orion glitters the brilliant star group of Taurus, northwest of the Hunter. Within Taurus are the two famous star clusters, Hyades (daughters of Atlas) and the Pleiades (also daughters of Atlas, although they are sometimes known as the seven sisters). The brightest star of the Hyades (and of Taurus itself) is Aldebaran (the follower) shining in the upper left-hand corner of the figure, which is shaped like the letter V. To the right of the Hyades is its neighboring cluster, Pleiades. Look for the seven sisters in autumn in the late evening, when the softly shining stars first appear. As winter advances, they become more brilliant.

Despite its name, the constellation is composed of many thousands of stars, their shining made more beautiful and mysterious because they are embedded in luminous nebula aglow with reflected starlight; the view through a telescope gives the impression of some lofty angelic city.

To the left of Orion glitters bright Gemini, neighbor to Taurus. Look toward its eastern boundary to find the Twins, Castor (tamer of horses) and Pollux (the pugilist). Castor is the mortal brother; the horses that it is his task to tame are the vibrant and rampant energies of his earthly nature. Pollux constantly taunts him to rise above his lower nature via the blows that goad us into a higher consciousness. It is interesting that, over the years, Pollux (the spirit) has become brighter, more powerful than Castor (the earth-bound man), although at one time Castor was the stronger star.

Faintly glimmering beneath Orion is Lepus, the Hare, its four brightest stars forming an irregular quadrilateral. The River Eridanus wends its starry way from close by the borders of Orion to meet the borders of the Whale (Cetus), thereon sweeping downward into the southern hemisphere.

Directly above Orion, and higher than Taurus and Gemini, shines Auriga (the Charioteer), forming the shape of an uneven pentagon in the skies. Capella, the Little Goat—Auriga's brightest star—is one of the most luminous in the heavens; it was discovered in 1900 to be a double star. Auriga is conceived of variously as a bearded man carrying a goat, a chariot and its rider, and a lame man riding a horse.

The Circumpolar Stars

The brightest star in the constellation of the Great Bear and the one directly below it are called "the pointers" because a straight line joining these two stars would point directly to the Pole Star. If you allow your eye to be guided by the pointers, you will recognize the Pole Star as the next noticeably brilliant star in line with them. The star seems as if it is stationary, the celestial point around which the others circle. It is the brightest star of the Little Bear (Ursa Minor).

On the side of the Pole Star, directly opposite the Plow (Ursa Major, or the Great Bear), is Cassiopeia, the Lady in the Chair. This is a clearly delineated constellation, smaller than the Plow but equally striking. The shape is a slightly irregular W, and its stars are particularly pure and radiant. Cassiopeia is deeply immersed in the pearly river of the Milky Way and was mother of the most brilliant temporary star in history, Tycho's Star, so called in honor of the sixteenth-century astronomer who carefully detailed its eighteen months of life; Tycho's Star was remarkable in that, at the height of its intensity, it was clearly visible in full daylight.

Capella of Auriga (the Charioteer) and Vega of the Lyre are also circumpolar stars, although their constellations are not.

Adjoining Cassiopeia to the right is Cepheus (named after Cepheus, King of Ethiopia, Cassiopeia's husband and Andromeda's father), four of its brightest stars forming a conspicuous trapezium. Its Delta star is the most brilliant of the class of variable stars known as cepheids.

WISEWOMAN'S JOURNAL

Skull Meditation

Uranus and Saturn are father and son, and old stories tell us that they were both gods of earth. Saturn has rulership over precious stones and the stony matter of the planet, and also over

skeletons—skulls and bones. It is good to commune with your skeleton, to feel it in your body, to soothe it and make it comfortable, and it is good to meditate upon your own skull. The skull is a magical symbol, and of itself it is a promise, a lesson, and an emblem of nourishment. Its promise is rebirth, for only through death may you be born again. The lesson it brings is that of the transitory nature of all things in material existence, for it is the fate of such things swiftly to pass away.

There is an eternal fixed smile upon the bony features of the naked skull, for it is its own essence, the structure of the world, and it knows that death is a kindly angel, assuring every man and woman, born to earth, life everlasting in the shining eternity of the god and goddess. Some say the smile is a grin, for the ancient and wise spirit of the skull is laughing at our dreary ideas of death. The whole pageant of life refutes our blind foolishness, if only we would look with inner eyes and listen with inner ears. Everywhere, throughout all nature, there is only the affirmation of life. This is the great lesson. The shape of the skull is at one with the shape of our mother planet, a symbol for being and consciousness, while its crossbones are the material universe, the four elements of which make up and structure matter. Behind the elements are the four great angels, and these are, to the north, Uriel or Sachiel and the gnomes, elves, and fairies; to the south, Michael and the salamanders (fire spirits, beings, and fairies); to the east, Raphael and the sylphs (fairies and spirits of the air); and to the west, Gabriel and the undines (water spirits and fairies, mermaids and tritons).

The skull and crossbones may be seen as the foursquare cross of matter resting in the divine circle of heavenly consciousness, represented by the skull. And so it is that the cross-within-the-circle is a most holy sign, stressing the cycle of the four great schools whose lessons are those of air (mind and thought), fire (inspiration, love, the heart), earth (steadfastness, stability, practicality, manifestation, and energy), and Water (the emotions and passions, the psyche, magical creativity, the-mind-in-the-heart). The cross-within-the-circle also affirms that the bones are the foundation of human, animal, and planetary life, the structure of the body itself, without which it would not be possible to plumb the mysterious depths and explore the treasury that is this miraculous realm of matter. The skeleton with its skull is the sacred sculpture of the body, and to commune with it is to commune with the angels.

As well as his rulership over structure, Saturn is Lord of Time. He directs the seconds, minutes, hours, days, weeks, and months of the year so that they form a sacred clock, the Clock of the Day and the Clock of the Year, for each day is a year in miniature, with its spring (morning), summer (afternoon), autumn (evening), and winter (night). The four Cross-Quarter Days mark the four great ancient festivals, and in the same way the hours of three, six, nine and twelve are holy and magical and are times for healing, prayer, meditation, communion with the god and the goddess and with the angels and the mystery at the heart of nature. At these hours it is good to find a stone and to sit with it in your hands, feeling its heartbeat and thinking of the heart of the earth, the mystic center of the mother planet that beats so that our own hearts keep time. To dwell often on the heart of Mother Earth is to heal her, to revere and bless her.

The New Year's Full Moon Lovespell

Upon the night of the first full moon of the year, go out in the evening and lean over the spars of the gates of a meadow or a stile. Look up at the moon and speak this charm:

All hail to thee, Luna! All hail to thee, Lady!
I pri'thee, good Moon, reveal to me
This night, whom it is my husband must be.

You must then bow very low to the moon three times and leave a bright sixpence upon the stile or the gate.* Hurry home and retire to bed directly, upon which your future spouse will visit you in your dreams.

Charm to Cure the Ague

Now the Doctrine of Signatures tells us that the aspen tree, with its delicate leaves all of a quiver, may cure the ague. You must ask the Spirit Lady of the tree to help you, and better it be if that is done upon the night of the full moon, being the night of the goddess.

Make a hole in the tree trunk, a very little one, smaller than a pecking bird would bore, and place within it some of your own nail parings, for these are a gift to the Lady; then fill up the hole, stuffing it well with moss and bark.

Now, shear a lock or a single curl from your head and pin it to the quaking leaves; for this too is an offering to the Lady.

Then you must sing, to a little melody of your own,

Aspen-tree, Aspen-tree,
I prithee
Shake and shiver instead of me.

Three times must you chant this rune, and three times must you bow to the Lady, to show faith and respect. Then bow once toward the moon, and homeward go, saying not a word until you are indoors. By the shining of the next full moon, your ague will have fled.

*If you have no sixpence, a glass bead will do.

The Book of Splendors

Now this is a good way to start the New Year. Keep beside you a book to write in, let it be a big book, but not too big. Bind it yourself if you can and, as you work, chant this rune:

> This book I bind, this book I bind
> All my heart's treasures to keep and find.

Now cover the front of the book, and its back, with a piece of cloth which you love, being embroidered and beautiful, and colored according to your tastes. As you work, chant this rune:

> This book I clothe, this book I clothe
> May all my dreams throughout be wove.

Call the first half to the middle the Book of Splendors and here record daily or at your convenience, those things in nature and in life that you see and perceive and which are lovely and precious to you: the delights of the skies, of the woods and copses, of the fields and meadows and hedgerows, of your garden and your home, of animals and children, of your workaday life, of your friends and your family, your travels and your rest, of the food you eat, of the things that you do and the things that you make, of the music you may hear, the books you may read, of the graceful things of art and cunning craft that you may look upon.

Let this be a book of Sunshine.

Call the second half the Book of Shadows and work it from the back through to the middle, as it is done in Araby. Record herein your nightly dreams, and those who speak to you through them. Record also the dreams of your heart, your heart's desires and its joys. Write down the teachings you receive as the gifts and the bounty of your workaday life. Write down those things your spirit yearns to know and to see. Write of your visions, and put these into poesy when you can, for that is good. Write of your mysteries, your magics, the deep and sequestered workings of your soul. Commune with the moon and the stars, and do not be afraid. Commune with the heart of our good Earth, for there is much to learn from the goddess and her Cauldron of Wonders. Make a seal from the things you love best in nature and imprint it upon your book.

Let this be a book of Secrets, and let it not be seen nor spoken of.

ISEWOMAN'S WEATHERBOOK

Look to the northern skies as evening falls, and if you see there a lurid ruddy glow as if there were some wickedness in it, be sure that there'll come a rush of blustery little breezes as cheeky as mill mice before the next moon rises.

When, in summertime, a hush steals over the land as if it had fainted away into a deep and dreamless sleep, and the air is so heavy you can scarce take a breath, that is the time when angry spirits are gathering, ready to fly into the breast of the world; be prepared for storms, for the heavens to be rent as if the Blast of Doom had been sounded, and for winds to rise that will make the house fire leap and charge up the chimney like a golden stag with the pack at its heels. Yet let not your heart be troubled; because after a great discharge of rain, the next day will dawn as fresh and smiling as a blue-eyed babe-in-arms.

Pigs can see the spirit of the wind, and can catch scent of it; if they rush about very excited, gripping bits of straw in their jaws, they are getting ready to welcome one of the company of the four winds; if they squeal more than is customary, and especially if they pierce the nighttime quiet with their uncanny demon-shrieks, you may look for the coming of a storm; but if they do no more than their wind dance, expect nothing more than a dry gusty wind full of friendly mischief.

❧

Look to the tops of the hills or to the far distances in the early morning before the first dews are gone; if a thick vapory mist you see, all wafting white like ghosts, take care to note whether it lingers, for that augurs rain and murk; and if it creeps toward you and turns gray as a monk's cowl, expect rum weather for a day or two; but if the sun sucks it up soon after dawn, then it'll turn out grand, fine and dry, for a good long spell.

❧

When the moon looks at you with ruddy cheeks, wait for the wind to get up and make a song and dance before it turns itself round again.

❧

When your cat is restless to the point of something uncanny, frisking about the house hither and thither as though Old Nick were after her, be assured that stormy bustling winds are on their way; when she sits all calm and quiet and blinking the peace of her wisdom into the fire, then you know the storm is about to blow itself out.

❧

When rooks fly overhead and make a right racket, they're letting you know that rain's on its way.

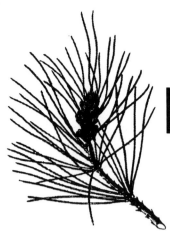

Chapter Twelve

FEBRUARY

Imbolc: The Rites of the Goddess

The Thunder, Perfect Mind

I was sent forth from the power,
  And I have come to those who reflect upon me,
  And I have been found among those who seek after me.
Look upon me, you who reflect upon me,
  And you hearers, hear me.
  You who are waiting for me, take me to yourselves.
And do not banish me from your sight.
  And do not make your voice hate me, nor
    your hearing.
  Do not be ignorant of me anywhere or any
    time. Be on your guard.
  Do not be ignorant of me.

For I am the first and the last,
I am the honoured one and the scorned one,
I am the whore and the holy one.
I am the wife and the virgin.

I am the mother and the daughter.
I am the members of my mother.
I am the barren one
  And many are her sons.
  And I have not taken a husband.
I am the midwife and she who does not bear.

I am the solace of my labour pains.
I am the bride and the bridegroom,
  And it is my husband who begot me.
I am the mother of my father
  And the sister of my husband,
  And he is my offspring.

I am the silence that is incomprehensible
  And the idea whose remembrance is frequent.
I am the voice whose sound is manifold
  And the word whose appearance is multiple.
I am the utterance of my name.

Gnostic text

NGELS, SPIRITS, AND STARS

Although each one of the twelve signs of the zodiac embodies a certain duality in its symbolism—or at least a counter-balancing influence—Pisces shares with Sagittarius and Gemini a pronounced duality. This duality provides a lesson in finding a point of balance and harmony between the manifest and the inner worlds, so that higher and lower consciousnesses may be attuned and work together. It is the sign of Jesus of Nazareth, master (or avatar) of the Piscean age. Pisces is associated with sacrificial service, secret enemies, monasteries, prison, exile, neuroses, confinement, seclusion, treachery, hospitals, and hidden motives. Its larger task is to wash away the fetters that bind each member of humanity to society's institutions and doctrines, to temporal authority and the rigidity of orthodox philosophy. This emotional, watery sign with its emphasis on the inner worlds of the soul must create the wine of the new dispensation so that Aquarius may pour it into the old wineskins that will give initial form to the new age. For this sacrificial sign, the symbol of the Nazarene giving his own blood in order to create the essential wine is one that is valid, however remote the degree of application, for each Piscean initiate.

Although most Pisceans must inevitably wrestle with this lunar-lit Night of the Soul, their compensation lies in the fact that the expansive, benign, and jovial Jupiter rules the sign in conjunction with mysterious

Neptune, god of the sea; so Pisces has dominion over the boundless ocean of creative life, the origin of all form that is given shape by the power of thought (Arthur Conan Doyle called it "a great sea of etheric impressions"). Jupiter asserts himself in Pisces as the god of freedom and the breaking of bonds. When his urges are denied full expression, their influence can lead to headlong escapism through drugs, alcohol, and dreams. Where Jupiter is obstructed, an effort to harmonize and counterbalance his fretful energies is necessary.

Although the watery signs of the zodiac have a tendency to merge into the background and so sacrifice the thrust of their individualistic consciousness, the rituals of baptism, initiation through water, can be seen as a rite for rescuing the drowned, raising them from the uterine waters of the etheric sea so that they might re-emerge into the sunlight of a new day, ready once more to pursue their individualism. The rite of baptism was one of the daily ceremonies of the Essene brothers, Hebrew priests who lived in communities throughout the northern desert (toward the River Jordan and the Red Sea); it signified purification and ritual rebirth . . . for life must come forth from the sea and walk upon the dry land. Such are the dictates of the stars, from the very beginning; this is a principle that applies equally to the higher spiritual worlds and to the physical earth—necessarily—for the latter is a reflection of the first but yet, also, its opposite, for all mirrors reverse the true image.

So the fishes of Pisces swim in opposite directions. The sigil is a picture of the physical reflecting the spiritual, its reversed image. That image hovers over the water, the Living Spirit, ready to be the Fisher of Men; and, as the two fishes of Pisces further depict, two choices confront the human fishes. They can rise to the bait of the Fisherman— or descend. If the fishes make the negative choice, the impulse of higher consciousness that is calling them out of the water becomes Neptune, the god who wields the Trident, symbol of the godhead— humanity's higher nature. The gentle rod has been required to transform itself into a spear.

In mythology, the god Neptune was called Poseidon by the Greeks. He was Saturn's eldest son. He was given dominion over the waves and lived in an underwater palace of dreamlike beauty, his subjects the mermaids and tritons of the waves. His staff was the Trident, associated with lightning, which he could employ to shake the earth to her foundations or to rule the turbulent, tossing waves of the secret, inner, hidden depths of the emotional, feeling life of humanity.

Neptune refines through dissolution. He is the god of formlessness and possibility, immaterial and subtle. He can deceive or reveal, according to the adjustment of the individual ego. He inspires artists and visionaries and drives the demon in those who become addicted to drugs and alcohol. His effects are general rather than individual, influencing generations and the tides that sweep and recede through the life of humanity. His energies are highly tuned, mysterious and supernatural.

Zodiac

PISCES—FISHES
FEBRUARY 19–MARCH 20

ANGELS: Sachiel and Asariel
RULING PLANETS: Jupiter, Neptune
KEYWORD: Privacy—the inner worlds, the realization of the individual triumphing over organized authority
AGE: 55–63 (age of wisdom, threshold of seniority)
METAL: Tin
CROSS: Mutable
ELEMENT: Water
QUALITIES: Intuitive, impressionable, fanciful, naive, free spirit, unworldly, creative, imaginative, clairvoyant, retiring, vulnerable, studious, romantic, emotional, trusting, vacillating, melancholy, indecisive, insecure, artistic
ILLNESSES TO GUARD AGAINST: Injury and ailments concerning the feet, chills, dropsy, malfunctioning liver, infectious diseases
BODY AREAS: Feet, toes
STONES: Sapphire, emerald, amethyst, coral, crystal, opal
NUMBERS: 3, 6
DAY: Thursday
FLOWERS AND HERBS: Heliotrope, carnation, opium poppy, violet

TREES: Willow, elm, linden tree (lime)
ANIMALS: Sheep, ox, seal
BIRDS: Swan, stork, sandpiper
COLORS: Purple, violet, amethyst, sea-green, turquoise

Piscean mythology relates how Venus and Cupid, in their flight from Typhon, leapt into the waters of the Euphrates, and were rescued from drowning by two fishes who were elevated to the heavens by the grateful goddess. This legend links Pisces with Capricorn, Saturn, and Aquarius. Capricorn stresses Christ-in-nature, and Aquarius must pour the Piscean Christ-wisdom into the old wineskins.

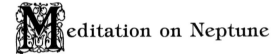

editation on Neptune

Light a green candle and dedicate it to Asariel,* Archangel of Neptune.

> Lord Neptune, I dwell upon your perfect spherical globe attended by your two moons and begin to conceive of your noble spirit, glowing in pearly glistening shades of aquamarine and rising in glory over the waves, your deep-fathomed domain. I pray that I may receive your aid in being given supernatural insights into the mysteries of life that lie just beyond the Veil; I ask that you bless me with the poetry of your inspiration so that I may express its subtle force harmoniously in all works of art that I undertake in my life, whether these be practical or visionary. Help me to dream vividly, to understand my dreams, and to be taken to the halls of spiritual wisdom and learning in my sleeping hours. Help me to recognize what is illusory and worthless in my life and to have the strength to turn decisively from it. Help me to develop my intuition so that I may know and perceive things that

---

* Asariel is not formally connected with any particular hour.

the intellect alone cannot grasp. Nurture within me
the powers of compassion and sharing that are yours.

Think of the spirit of Neptune clothed in his etheric robes of
amethyst, violet, and sea-green and feel his influences surrounding you
as you watch the candle burn down.

Stars of Winter

Perseus, the great hero of old who rescued Andromeda as she
waited, chained to a rock, for a great sea-monster to devour her, appears
in the heavens as a brilliant constellation to the right of Auriga, farther
along the celestial river of the Milky Way. It may be recognized by its
virtually equilateral triangle, marked by three bright stars with a
fainter one glimmering at its heart. A beautiful stream of brilliant stars
is the second notable feature in Perseus.

Look for Beta Persei, or Algol (demon or ghoul), the "winking star";
the Demon shines brightly for about two and a half days (the period in
which the moon remains in each sign of the zodiac in her monthly
round), after which it appears to go out, glistening dimly for about
fifteen minutes, and then regains its lustre within nine hours, a number
sacred to the moon. It is in this nine-hour period that she advances to
her new zodiacal sign. This apparent sympathy with lunar magic may
have inspired the Arabs to give the star its name. The Demon appears
to be fading when it mysteriously retreats from the solar system and
travels back toward us when its luster begins to reestablish itself; in
this respect it behaves like the moon-ruled tides of the sea.

The first star of Perseus, Alpha Persei, or Mirfak (elbow), shines at
the heart of a remarkable region of the skies. Mirfak is festooned with
stars gleaming like a precious bracelet around the "elbow"; their
arrangement is so pronounced in its symmetry that it seems possible
that they are truly physically linked, veritable heavenly jewelry.

Close to the margin of Casseopeia shines the star Che Persei.
Nearby, the marvelous double duster in Perseus may be found. It is just
a misty ring of milky light to the naked eye, but through a telescope it
may be seen in all its glory.

The Circumpolar Stars

Adjoining Cepheus, in which the beautiful star Mu Cephei shines red as a precious stone, justifying Herschel's naming of it as the "garnet star," Draco meanders along the celestial way near the Great Bear, and ends in a line of stars parallel to that part of the Bear that is commonly called the Plow. Three of its most radiant stars form a diamond-shaped figure near the boundaries of the constellation Hercules.

To watch the revolutions of the circumpolar stars is to watch the motion of our own earth projected on to the great cosmic sphere. These Silent Watchers of the Heavens are always with us, and to establish a familiarity with them is to begin to know a deep sense of peace, eternity, and serene well-being. My grandmother, Sarah Greaves, said: "The tranquil stars of heaven shine from above like jewels, but the precious stones of the Earth are buried far and deep." The contemplation of this truth gives birth to the answering echo that the treasury of stars, as they shine from the skies, imparts a golden inspiration to bring forth humanity's greatest and most precious jewel, which resides as a flame, a seed of the spirit, in the human heart.

 ISEWOMAN'S JOURNAL

Dreams and Visions

To dream of the wind as it rushes through the night brings a letter or a communication by token or symbol; look to the spirit that drives you and, in your waking hours, listen to the spirit-voices in the wind, for there is meaning and wisdom in them. To dream of rapid waters, clear and pure, betokens an enrichment of life, new vigor in your fortunes, an enhancing of your will and power of direction. Do not dissipate your life force. Do not lose control. Something joyful in you seeks release and finds freedom. Be glad of heart and find earthly waters, moving or still, to walk by and meditate upon. Then you shall taste the fruit of your dreams. If in your nightly visions you have seen rough and unquiet waters, something in your life needs cleansing; do not bemoan your fate as destiny fulfills itself, for this purging is good and godly and will bring a source of renewal into your life that is deep and beautiful, like a well with a star in it.

To dream of flowers brings joy and delight and angelic blessings. A crocus in your dreams bears this message: walk in sunlit ways and do not be distracted by shadows and benighted paths; a daffodil: a friend nurses some hurt, offer him or her the treasures of your heart and understanding; a violet: your spouse will be youthful in thought and attitude throughout life; a snowdrop: do not enfold your secret hopes in your breast, but share them with a trusted and sympathetic friend.

If you should see catkins in a dream, this pretty spring burgeoning counsels you in dream-wisdom that there is gold and much that is precious in your life; but it hangs on the tree, it is not for gathering. You must summon your soul to become aware of it, or you will pass it by unheeding; and, in becoming aware of it, you will rejoice in its fruitfulness and revel in its bounty, because the nature of this golden treasury is that it cannot be spent; that is the secret of its joy and your dream's message. A simplification of this would be to say "count your blessings."

To dream of a hare is sometimes a warning. Fleet of foot and graceful, this lovely animal courses through your dreams to alert you to the ill-wishes and machinations of those who would hurt you or bring misfortune on your family. Be brave of heart and act with firmness of purpose to turn around the evil when it appears, and good will come out of it. If the hare is distressed in its running, so says this dream to you; but if the creature gambols and sports and runs in joy, you may take it that the hare has appeared in its true guise as herald of the returning spring, and you may be glad, indeed; for fresh strength and hope, new beginnings, and the blossoming of promises will restore your spirit.

To dream of a lamb is lucky and denotes peace and well-being, wisdom, and blessings. It signifies fertility, whether this be material plenty, artistic inspiration, or the conceiving of a child.

To dream of a lion is to know that providence has decreed that you are to be given power. If the lion attacks, you are counseled to consult your conscience when you receive it to be sure of not abusing it; but if the lion be amongst, or leader of, a pride, or walks, runs, or lies majestically and unaroused, the power that shall soon be yours, in whatever sphere, shall bring benediction and beautify your life. To dream of a dandelion, a kingcup, a celandine or indeed any yellow flower is a sign that you must seek to empower yourself to bring the sun down into your earthly life, perhaps because you have been neglecting to heal some hurt or inharmonious condition; but it also says to you that there is gold at the heart of all things, and smiles behind tears.

To dream of a frog is propitious; it signifies material success, profits for the trader, generous crops for the farmer, benediction on the traveler, conquests for the adventurer, and a joyful wedding for the lover. This little green-coated man haunts ponds and ferny pools like a spirit and brings leaping life up from the silent depths. He wears the color of the fairies and is beneficent and wholesome.

To dream of a unicorn is a blessed dream indeed. To dream of unicorns dancing is to know that some great spiritual purpose is to be revealed in your life; to dream of these mystic creatures together with their foals is to know that you will be the initiator of some wonderful happiness either for yourself or another, and that the fruits of the past are to be brought forth in splendor. And to dream of them singing is to know that you will be entrusted with precious spiritual powers for the healing and enlightenment of those around you.

WISEWOMAN'S WEATHERBOOK

If you hear the call of the curlew over and over again, as though a spirit were singing, you are hearing the voice of the Gabriel Hounds behind it; and you shall know that a storm is brewing, as if it were called up by witches.

When gulls flock far inland, there are storms at sea, and soon they will be hurrying after the seabirds and discharging their fury over terra firma; this is why gulls are harbingers of evil weather and messengers of the storm.

If you should see waxwings massing in great numbers, as though holding counsel from all over the wide world, these country birds foretell, for the future of that year, harsh weather, bitter cold, poor health, and strange diseases, and sinister stirrings in the affairs of the world. Take heed of this sign, and do all you can to safeguard your health and to promote peace among your fellows.

Charm to Turn Away Violent and Dangerous Weather

When the snow falls deep and thick and gathers into perilous drifts, or yet when the winds seem to spin themselves into a tornado as if they would wreak havoc, or when the rains flood as if they were a biblical plague, hurling down hail and presaging thunder and lightning, you may chant this rune to the Strangers (that is, the fairies, or the Little People). Say it aloud and out of doors, even should that be just on your own doorstep; and mind you respect the fairies, or you cannot hope to gain their trust.

Angels Four we call upon
Of Air and Earth and Moon and Sun;
And fairies too we call upon,
Of sky and land and sea and fire,
May fairies give ear to our desire;
Calm the wind, soothe the storm
Let the raindrops cease to form;
To hush the thunder, clear the skies
We chant this rune both good and wise;
And by our Holy Lord and Lady
So mote it be; so mote it be.

Charm to Stop the Rain

Say aloud to the teeming skies:

Rain, rain, go away,
Come again tomorrow day;
When I brew and when I bake,
I'll give you a little cake.

If, in a little while, it rains still, you must bake a little oaten cake and leave it on your doorstep for the rain-spirit, for that will please our Lady, who rules him. Bless the cake, and give it in great reverence.

When the moon's on its back in the winter skies, there'll be a nipping frost, and air as cold as the shroud, while the stars will shine as if washed with dew. When the moon-boat tilts in the spring, expect weather fair and radiant as a bride, shining with a brightness and vivacity not seen in any other season.

*The Tree of Life**

Come with me down into the deep secret places of the Earth, down deep into her Heart. Here there is a great Light that glows like no outer sun but rather blazes with a spiritual light so pure and lovely that mortal eye may behold it only in dreams and visions of the soul. It is the brilliant effulgence of Love and Joy, the supreme radiance of the godhead.

Here in the earth's heart it is as if we stand in a fragrant garden; and in the garden there grows a Tree. It is the Tree of Life. We may go to it and stand at its roots, locked firmly into the stuff of Mother Earth. In wonder we gaze up into its boughs, garlanded with leaves tenderly glowing with a soft, peaceful green hue and hung with fruits of heavenly, sparkling colors shimmering with the luster of the stars. Rainbow-colored birds come and go among its branches, as do little beasts of gentle dun earth shades and strange mythic animals whose fabulous color and form we have never seen or imagined before. Each one speaks to our heart and is our brother. In joyous commun-

---

* Imbolc was associated with the purification of Mother Earth as her rites of preparation before receiving the divine fires of the spring; her secret, invisible magic was at its strongest as the hidden seeds stirred in her depths. The "Tree of Life" meditation is an old method of purifying the psyche.

ion we greet one another, and our voices rise in song, for it is the morning of the new day.

Yes, the dawn is breaking, and, as we look up, further and deeper into the mysteries of the Tree, we see that there are many paths upward into its boughs, as though it were all at once a Tree and a Mountain and a Dream. With joy our hearts take wing because we see that, at its very summit, the light of the Godhead streams forth and pours downward like a bright river of Paradise deep into the heart of the earth where we stand, and into our own heart-vessels and into the world of sorrow above.

Then in a vision within a vision, we see ourselves clambering upward upon one of the paths that lead from the roots, up to the heavens where the angels choir in a wonder of bliss to help and inspire us on our struggling upward way. With the Staff of Life, the Pouch of Provisions, and the Undying Lantern we climb, and we are never alone. Around us, all upon their own elected paths, we see the sons and daughters of humanity ascending likewise; but we are all linked in a network of light.

Then we are alone again, with just the peaceful Tree stretching above us, waving its beautiful branches over our head in benediction. Soothed, we dwell upon its shelter and protection, its kindly power and strength, the motherly fragrance of its fruits and flowers, the lullabies in its rustling leafsongs.

Refreshed and glad of heart, we stroke the bark of the Tree and feel its goodness, its wholeness. Comforted, healed, and ready for renewed service, we seek once more the world above, taking with us the vivifying light of the new day.

INDEX